VEGAN,
at Times

**Also by
Jessica Seinfeld**

*Food Swings: 125+
Recipes to Enjoy Your Life
of Virtue and Vice*

*The Can't Cook Book:
100+ Recipes for the
Absolutely Terrified!*

*Double Delicious!: Good,
Simple Food for Busy,
Complicated Lives*

*Deceptively Delicious:
Simple Secrets to
Get Your Kids Eating
Good Food*

VEGAN, at Times

120+ RECIPES
for Every Day or Every So Often

Jessica Seinfeld

WITH **SARA QUESSENBERRY**

GALLERY BOOKS

New York   London   Toronto   Sydney   New Delhi

Gallery Books
An Imprint of Simon & Schuster, Inc.
1230 Avenue of the Americas
New York, NY 10020

First Gallery Books hardcover edition October 2021

GALLERY BOOKS and colophon are registered
trademarks of Simon & Schuster, Inc.

For information about special discounts for bulk purchases,
please contact Simon & Schuster Special Sales at
1-866-506-1949 or business@simonandschuster.com.

The Simon & Schuster Speakers Bureau can bring authors
to your live event. For more information or to book an event,
contact the Simon & Schuster Speakers Bureau at
1-866-248-3049 or visit our website at www.simonspeakers.com.

Interior design by Laura Palese

Manufactured in China

10 9 8 7 6 5 4 3 2 1

Library of Congress Cataloging-in-Publication Data

Names: Seinfeld, Jessica, author. | Quessenberry, Sara, author.
Title: Vegan, at times : 120+ easy recipes for every day or every
so often / Jessica Seinfeld with Sara Quessenberry.
Description: New York, NY : Gallery Books, [2021] | Includes index.
Identifiers: LCCN 2021004660 (print) | LCCN 2021004661 (ebook)
| ISBN 9781982149574 (board) | ISBN 9781982149598 (ebook)
Subjects: LCSH: Vegan cooking. | Cooking
(Natural foods) | LCGFT: Cookbooks.
Classification: LCC TX837 .S385 2021 (print) |
LCC TX837 (ebook) | DDC 641.5/6362—dc23
LC record available at https://lccn.loc.gov/2021004660
LC ebook record available at https://lccn.loc.gov/2021004661

ISBN 978-1-9821-4957-4
ISBN 978-1-9821-4959-8 (ebook)

To my mom, Ellen, who forced our family to eat tofu and brown rice before it was cool. To my daughter, Sascha, whose resistance to healthy food has kept me working like a fool. I am grateful to you both.

Introduction

I love to try new things. I love to experiment. I don't mind when something doesn't work.

Kitchens and food are just a giant playground to me. I love lots of things you won't find in the strict vegan diet. I love cheese. I love honey. But, hey: you picked up this book. It means you're not a strict rule-follower. Neither am I.

Humans love variety. Sometimes we eat healthy and at times we don't. At times we can commit to a marathon, and at times we are content with walks in the park. At times we have the willpower to lose those extra pounds, at times we can't stop eating. That's a fact of life. This is also a fact: if you eat vegan food a few days a week, you will feel better, have more energy, do good for animals and the planet. And experience that warm glow of accomplishment from having changed your eating habits.

I've written five cookbooks; they each have a problem-solving theme. This one is no different. In this book, you still have permission to do what you want, when you want. These pages will not shame you, because, as always, to me there is nothing more annoying and self-important than food shaming.

Most recipes in this book don't require advanced planning. The ingredients are easy to find at mainstream grocery stores, and even on Amazon. The recipes are simple to follow and are friendly to those who are skeptics, who are on a budget, or who are not necessarily a natural in the kitchen.

I was a skeptic, too. So was my husband. When veganism started to be a thing, we were turned off by its image. It seemed too dogmatic and smug. But, my friend Camilla, who owns a big farm (and is also a devoted cat mother), finally got to me: when we had dinner one night, it was obvious to me she felt way better and more energized after her dinner veggies and grains than I did from my burger. She convinced me in the moment that it was not only about taking care of our bodies and the planet but also about being good to animals. I wholeheartedly agree with all three of these tenets of veganism, but I wasn't fully convinced I could sustain this lifestyle.

I started to eat vegan, at times, and I began to feel the difference. When I ate that way, I slept better and had more energy when I was awake. And it opened up a new world of options. I notice a difference when I eat the right things versus the wrong things. However, I am also ready to have a good steak once in a while. I admit it. (I'm ready for your wrath, too, some of you.)

And that's the point. After eating vegan, at times, for a while, you might start to dither on dairy, and not be able to look a rib eye in the eye. And you might enjoy the whole new world of eating that opens up.

It's time to eat, enjoy, and live your life without fear of judgment. Find the ingredients you need where you already shop, and be among fellow adventurers who are curious about vegan food, but are also not ready to give up their love of cheese, eggs, and those other "non-vegan" items. With all we've got going on in today's world, food should stand above as a pleasure and a delight.

Think of it as being in my kitchen. Be curious. Be adventurous. If you're ready, I officially invite you to be a Vegan, at Times.

Pantry

Here is a list of ingredients frequently used
throughout this book for you to have on hand in your
pantry. You are probably familiar with,
or have at least heard of, most of them—and hopefully
they don't scare you. These ingredients are
easy to find and affordable. We purposely shopped
at mainstream grocery stores and big
price-conscious retailers to develop the recipes
here. Buy at your own pace.

BASICS

Hot sauce

Sriracha

Barbecue sauce

Lower-sodium tamari and/or
   lower-sodium soy sauce

Pure maple syrup

Canned whole and diced tomatoes

Tomato paste

Canned chipotle peppers in adobo

Dijon mustard

Peanut butter

Tahini

Jam and/or preserves

Nutritional yeast

Dry white wine

SPICES

Ground cumin

Ground coriander

Smoked paprika

Paprika

Curry powder

Crushed red pepper flakes

Chili powder

Chipotle powder

Cayenne pepper

Ground cinnamon

Whole nutmeg

Dried oregano

Granulated onion

Bay leaves

Kosher salt (We like
   Diamond Crystal)

Flaky sea salt

Whole black peppercorns

OILS AND VINEGARS

Extra virgin olive oil

Coconut oil

Toasted sesame oil

Red wine vinegar

White wine vinegar

Apple cider vinegar

Unseasoned rice vinegar

PRODUCE

Onions (red, yellow, and white)

Shallots

Scallions

Garlic

Ginger

Potatoes (sweet and Yukon Gold)

Fresh herbs

Lemons and limes

PASTAS AND GRAINS

Short and long pastas

Quinoa

Farro

Basmati rice (brown or white)

Jasmine rice (brown or white)

Millet

BEANS AND LEGUMES

Chickpeas

Black beans

Cannellini beans

Lentils

NUTS AND SEEDS

Almonds (roasted and blanched)

Peanuts (roasted)

Cashews (roasted and raw)

Walnuts

Pine nuts

Chia seeds

Sunflower seeds

Roasted pepitas (pumpkin seeds)

Sesame seeds

Hemp hearts

Flaxseeds and flaxseed meal

"DAIRY"

Milk, such as cashew, oat, and almond

Unsweetened coconut milk

Shredded cheddar (We like Violife)

Cream cheese (We like Violife and Kite Hill)

Butter (We like Miyoko's)

Yogurt (coconut, almond, or cashew)

BAKING

All-purpose flour

Granulated sugar

Confectioners' sugar

Dark brown sugar

Unsweetened shredded coconut

Sweetened flake coconut

Cocoa powder

Dark chocolate chips (vegan)

Old-fashioned rolled oats

Baking powder

Baking soda

Cornstarch

Pure vanilla extract

Dried fruit

Nonstick vegetable oil cooking spray

Helpful Kitchen Equipment:

MULTIPURPOSE EQUIPMENT

Food processor (11-cup)

Blender

Chef's knife

Paring knife

Serrated knife

Cutting boards

Dutch oven (5½-quart)

Large pot with lid (8-quart)

Medium saucepan with lid (3-quart)

Small saucepan with lid (2-quart)

Small, medium, and large skillets (8-inch, 10-inch, 12-inch)

Nonstick skillets (8-inch, 10-inch, 12-inch)

Tongs

Wooden spoons

Whisk

Silicone spatula

Metal spatula

Vegetable peeler

Microplane and/or box grater

Citrus juicer

Measuring cups and spoons

Colander and/or strainer

Rimmed sheet pans (18 x 13-inch)

Pepper mill

BAKING EQUIPMENT

Electric mixer

Wire cooling rack

12-cup muffin tin

Loaf pan (8½ x 4½-inch)

9-inch round cake pan

8-inch square baking pan

9 x 13-inch baking dish

9-inch pie plate

CHAPTER ONE

Breakfast

Sweet Oat Crepes

Can a dairy-free pancake look and taste this magnificent?
The answer is: Yes.

Active: 30 min / Total: 30 min / Makes 14 crepes

---

1 cup all-purpose flour, spooned and leveled

1 cup oat flour, spooned and leveled

½ teaspoon kosher salt

2⅓ cups unsweetened plant-based milk, such as oat, cashew, or almond

¼ cup unsweetened apple sauce

2 teaspoons pure vanilla extract

3½ teaspoons coconut oil

1½ cups of your favorite jam

Confectioners' sugar, for dusting

Fresh berries, for serving

Heat the oven to 225°F.

In a medium bowl, whisk together the all-purpose flour, oat flour, and salt. Whisk in half of the milk at a time. Then whisk in the apple sauce and vanilla.

In an 8-inch nonstick skillet, heat ¼ teaspoon of the oil over medium heat.

Scoop out a scant ¼ cup batter. With one hand, lift up the skillet and swirl it in a circular motion as you pour the batter in with your other hand to get a thin, round crepe. (It usually takes one or two crepes to get the temperature of the skillet just right.) Cook for about 1½ minutes, or until the underside is light golden brown. Then use a spatula to flip it. Cook for about 30 seconds more. Slide it onto a plate and keep warm in the oven while you make the remaining crepes.

To fill the crepes, thinly spread about 2 tablespoons jam over each crepe and roll up. Dust the crepes with confectioners' sugar and serve with berries.

Yogurt with Warm Blueberry Compote

Warm, sweet fruit atop your favorite yogurt is a (nutritious) jolt of lightning in the morning. Or whenever it strikes you.

Active: 5 min / Total: 15 min / Serves 4

6-ounce package fresh (or frozen) blueberries (about 1¼ cups)

2 tablespoons fruit preserves or jam, such as apricot or strawberry

3 tablespoons fresh orange juice or water

2 cups coconut or cashew yogurt

½ cup chopped roasted almonds

¼ cup hemp hearts

2 tablespoons chia seeds

In a small saucepan, combine the blueberries, preserves, and orange juice over medium-high heat and let come to a boil. Reduce the heat to medium and simmer for 3 to 5 minutes, stirring occasionally, until the blueberries start to break down and the sauce thickens slightly. Remove from the heat and let cool for a few minutes.

Divide the yogurt, almonds, hemp hearts, and chia seeds among bowls. Spoon in the warm compote.

Fluffy Pancakes

These are easy but decadent and a nice example of how doable and delicious vegan life can be. Care to join us?

Active: 20 min / Total: 20 min / Makes 14 pancakes

2 cups all-purpose flour, spooned and leveled

4 teaspoons baking powder

½ teaspoon baking soda

1¼ teaspoons kosher salt

1½ cups plus 2 tablespoons unsweetened plant-based milk, such as cashew, oat, or almond

2 tablespoons pure maple syrup, plus more for serving

2 teaspoons apple cider vinegar

2 teaspoons pure vanilla extract

Coconut oil, for cooking

In a medium bowl, whisk together the flour, baking powder, baking soda, and salt.

In a liquid measuring cup, measure the milk, then stir in the maple syrup, vinegar, and vanilla. Add to the dry ingredients and gently whisk to combine (a few lumps are okay).

Heat a large nonstick skillet or griddle over medium-high heat until it's nice and hot. Then reduce the heat to medium-low. For each batch of pancakes, melt 1 to 2 teaspoons of oil and swirl to coat the bottom of the skillet.

Scoop the batter (¼ cup per pancake) into the skillet, spacing the pancakes 2 inches apart. Cook for 1 to 2 minutes, until bubbles form on top and start to burst and the undersides are golden brown. Flip the pancakes and cook for 1 to 2 minutes more, until golden and puffed.

Warm the maple syrup and serve with the pancakes.

Chocolate Banana Bread

This was the first vegan item in our house that was unanimously approved. Full disclosure: they did not, still do not, know it is vegan. Chopping a chunk of chocolate is fancier; using chocolate chips is easier. Your choice.

Active: 15 min / Total: 1 hr 15 min (plus cooling time) / Serves 8

Nonstick vegetable oil cooking spray

¾ cup walnuts

1½ cups mashed ripe bananas (about 3 large)

¾ cup sugar

½ cup extra virgin olive oil

1 teaspoon pure vanilla extract

2 cups all-purpose flour, spooned and leveled

1½ teaspoons baking powder

½ teaspoon baking soda

¾ teaspoon kosher salt

¾ teaspoon ground cinnamon

½ cup chopped dark chocolate (or chips; vegan), plus more for the top

Heat the oven to 350°F. Spray an 8½ x 4½-inch loaf pan with cooking spray. Line with parchment paper, leaving an overhang on the two long sides (for lifting out the baked bread).

Spread the walnuts on a sheet pan and bake for about 10 minutes, or until fragrant and crisp. Let them cool, then coarsely chop.

In a large bowl, whisk together the bananas, sugar, oil, and vanilla. Add the flour, baking powder, baking soda, salt, and cinnamon and stir to combine (the batter will be thick). Fold in the chocolate and walnuts.

Scrape the batter into the prepared pan and smooth the top. Sprinkle the top with some more shards of chocolate.

Bake for 57 to 60 minutes, until a toothpick inserted into the center comes out with a few moist crumbs attached. Let cool on a wire cooling rack for 20 minutes before unmolding. Let cool completely before slicing.

Tofu Salsa Scramble Breakfast Burrito

For those of us missing eggs in the morning,
this will substitute nicely.

Active: 10 min / Total: 10 min / Serves 4

1 tablespoon extra virgin olive oil

One 14-ounce package firm tofu,
drained and patted dry

½ cup of your favorite jarred salsa

Four 8- to 10-inch flour tortillas

1 avocado, sliced

16 cherry or grape tomatoes,
quartered

Fresh cilantro leaves, for serving

Kosher salt and freshly ground black
pepper, for serving

Hot sauce, for serving

In a medium nonstick skillet, heat the oil over medium-high heat. Crumble the tofu into the skillet. Cook for 2 to 3 minutes, stirring occasionally, until hot and any water has cooked away. Stir in the salsa and cook for 1 to 2 minutes, until heated through.

To heat the tortillas, turn the flame on your stove to medium-high. Using tongs, grab a tortilla and drag it over the burner grate, flipping it, until lightly charred on both sides but still pliable. Repeat. (Alternatively, heat the tortillas in a dry medium skillet over medium-high heat.)

Fill each tortilla with the tofu scramble, avocado, tomatoes, and cilantro. Sprinkle with a little salt and pepper and shake on some hot sauce. Roll up like a burrito.

Spicy Tomato Juice

Sometimes you need a spicy and satisfying reset to change your brain.

Active: 5 min   /   Total: 5 min   /   Serves 1

1 medium beefsteak tomato, cored and quartered

1 red bell pepper, cored, seeded, and quartered

1 tablespoon fresh lemon juice

A few dashes of Tabasco

½ teaspoon Old Bay seasoning or celery salt

Put the tomato and bell pepper in a blender with the lemon juice, Tabasco, and Old Bay. Blend until smooth.

Honeydew-Cucumber-Mint Juice

Sweet melon combined with spicy ginger and fresh mint is my kind of party these days.

Active: 5 min   /   Total: 5 min   /   Serves 1

½ cucumber, peeled

1 cup honeydew melon pieces

1 cup fresh baby spinach

1 tablespoon fresh lime juice

2 teaspoons grated peeled fresh ginger

6 fresh mint leaves

3 tablespoons coconut milk

Cut the cucumber into large chunks and put in a blender with the honeydew, spinach, lime juice, ginger, mint, and coconut milk. Blend until smooth.

Pressure Cooker Porridge with Toasted Almonds and Jam

A great breakfast for a busy household or a delicious brunch
when a vegan is joining. Millet is rich in nutrients,
gluten-free, mild in flavor, and filling.

Active: 10 min / Total: 40 min / Serves 4 to 6

1 cup millet

2 cups water, plus more if necessary

2 cups unsweetened plant-based milk, such as cashew, oat, or almond

1 tablespoon dark brown sugar

1 teaspoon pure vanilla extract

⅛ teaspoon kosher salt

½ cup sliced almonds

Fruit in season, such as pomegranate seeds or peaches

Jam, for serving

In a pressure cooker, combine the millet, water, milk, brown sugar, vanilla, and salt. Pressure cook on high for 10 minutes. Let the pressure release naturally for 15 minutes, then carefully open the vent to release the remaining steam.

While the millet cooks, put the almonds in a small skillet over medium heat. Cook for 3 to 5 minutes, tossing often, until golden brown.

Serve the porridge topped with the almonds, fruit, and a spoonful of jam.

For the stovetop: In a large saucepan, combine 1 cup millet, 3 cups water, 2 cups milk, 1 tablespoon brown sugar, 1 teaspoon vanilla, and ⅛ teaspoon salt over medium-high heat and let come to a boil. Reduce the heat to medium-low, cover partially with a lid, and simmer, stirring occasionally, for 40 to 50 minutes, until the millet is creamy and tender. You might have to add up to ½ cup more water if it becomes too thick.

Peanut Butter Granola

Eat with your favorite milk, top off your yogurt or porridge,
or keep it on the counter for visitors.

Active: 5 min / Total: 40 min / Makes 4 cups

2 cups old-fashioned rolled oats

1 cup roasted salted peanuts

½ cup flaxseeds

¼ cup peanut butter powder

¼ cup pure maple syrup

2 tablespoons coconut sugar or dark brown sugar

2 tablespoons coconut oil

2 teaspoons pure vanilla extract

1 teaspoon kosher salt

Fresh or dried fruit, for serving

Unsweetened plant-based milk or yogurt, for serving

Heat the oven to 300°F. Line a rimmed sheet pan with parchment paper.

In a large bowl, combine the oats, peanuts, and flaxseeds.

In a small skillet, combine the peanut butter powder, maple syrup, coconut sugar, oil, vanilla, and salt over medium-low heat. Whisk until creamy and smooth.

Pour the peanut butter mixture over the oat mixture. Use a silicone spatula to stir until well combined and the oats are evenly coated.

Scrape the mixture into the prepared pan and spread out into an even layer.

Bake for about 35 minutes, stirring halfway through, or until crisp.

Serve with fresh or dried fruit and milk or yogurt.

Flaky Biscuits

These biscuits are shocking. They are so tender and flaky
that they could be a catalyst for any nonbeliever.

Active: 15 min / Total: 40 min / Makes 9 biscuits

3 cups all-purpose flour, spooned
and leveled, plus more for rolling

¼ cup sugar

1 tablespoon baking powder

¼ teaspoon baking soda

2 teaspoons kosher salt

1 cup (8 ounces) plant-based butter
(We like Miyoko's), cut into small
pieces and frozen for about 10
minutes

½ cup plus 1 to 3 tablespoons
unsweetened plant-based milk,
such as cashew, oat, or almond

1 teaspoon apple cider vinegar

Flaky sea salt, for the tops

Jam or preserves, for serving

Heat the oven to 400°F. Line a sheet pan with parchment paper.

In a food processor, pulse together the flour, sugar, baking powder,
baking soda, and salt. Add the butter pieces and pulse a few times,
until the butter pieces are the size of peas; they don't have to be
uniform. Pour the mixture into a large bowl.

In a liquid measuring cup, combine the ½ cup milk and the vinegar.
Pour over the dry ingredients. Using a fork, gently stir together to
incorporate. The mixture should be moist (not wet) and a little shaggy
(but not dry). Add the 1 to 3 tablespoons milk, a tablespoon at a time, if
necessary.

Sprinkle your work surface with a little flour and pour out the mixture.
Gather up the loose mixture and gently press it together into a 1-inch-
thick roughly shaped rectangle. Fold it in half over itself (this will help
form the layers), adding any stray pieces to the top. Now gently knead
the dough to bring it together, then shape it into a fat disk a little over
1 inch thick.

Using a 2½-inch-wide biscuit cutter or glass, press straight down
(without twisting the cutter) to form the biscuits. Flip the biscuits
upside down (this will give them a sharp edge) and place on the
prepared pan. Reshape the scraps and cut them out, too. Sprinkle the
tops with a little sea salt.

Bake for 12 minutes, then rotate the pan. Bake for 8 to 10 minutes more,
until the undersides are golden brown and the tops are browned at the
edges. Serve warm with jam.

Chia Pudding with Caramelized Bananas

The chia pudding is a great staple to keep in the fridge, and you will make these caramelized bananas over and over again and put them on everything. Consider the French Toast on page 33.

Active: 15 min / **Total: 15 min** / **Serves 2**

4 tablespoons chia seeds

⅔ cup unsweetened plant-based milk, such as cashew, oat, or almond

2 small bananas

4 teaspoons dark brown sugar

2 teaspoons coconut oil

¼ cup toasted unsweetened coconut chips

In a small bowl, combine the chia seeds and milk. Let stand, stirring occasionally, for 12 to 15 minutes, until pudding-like.

Meanwhile, slice the bananas on the diagonal about ½ inch thick. Put in a medium bowl, sprinkle with the brown sugar, and stir to coat.

In a medium nonstick skillet, heat the oil over medium heat. Place the banana slices in a single layer in the skillet so they lie flat. Let cook for 1 to 2 minutes, until the undersides are golden brown and caramelized. Flip the banana slices over and cook for 1 to 2 minutes more.

Divide the chia pudding between the bowls and top with the bananas and coconut chips.

Liberate
Yourself

As I embrace the winter of my youth, I find what I eat and drink has a real impact on how I feel. It took me awhile to figure this out.

When I was younger, I could easily consume a huge meal of steak, french fries, wine, and dessert and feel fine. In my forties, I started to feel hungover the next morning. I wasn't drinking *that* much wine. So what was it? It was the food. I realized that what I ate could either drain me or invigorate me.

I began to experiment, cutting back on meat and dairy. I didn't make any promises to myself or anybody else. I didn't even tell anybody else. This was something I was doing alone, something for me. And, gradually, my body responded. I slept better, I had more energy and fewer aches and pains, my digestion improved, and I even lost a few pounds.

Now, the vegans I had come across at that time were a bossy bunch, always yelling that their way was the only way. To me, the turnoff wasn't making the big jump to a new way of eating; it was the way some vegans made everyone else feel terrible for eating meat and dairy.

Was I going to become one of those people, sermonizing while listeners' eyes rolled back in their heads with tedium? At a large dinner party I once attended, a man regaled the table with his story about how easy it was to become a vegan. On and on he went, not noticing that the rest of us were slack-jawed at his arrogance in taking over the meal with his new lifestyle. I thought to myself, if I ever did consider this way of eating, I would keep it to myself.

So, I slowly and quietly migrated toward eating less dairy and meat, without putting a label on it. I instead decided to be brandless, label-less in my current independent state. I liberated myself from any category, and so I was free to change my mind about how I eat. I owned my appetite and my choices.

It dawned on me that this might be a brand in itself: someone who is noncommittal about putting a stake (not a steak!) in the ground about how they eat. Someone who weighs the respectful opinions of others but might have a piece of cheese while considering how to contribute in meaningful ways. I love cheese. I know there are many reasons to not eat cheese, but I don't want to be shamed if, at times, I want to eat cheese.

Whatever we call ourselves, it's time to liberate from the shame around food. That's how we really get healthy in this world.

Was I going to become one of those people, sermonizing while listeners' eyes rolled back in their heads with tedium?

Chickpea Pancakes

A savory, gluten-free brunch option for you.

Active: 20 min / Total: 20 min / Serves 4

1½ cups plus 2 tablespoons chickpea flour, spooned and leveled

2 tablespoons chopped fresh dill, plus more for serving

3 scallions (white and light green parts), chopped

¾ teaspoon kosher salt, plus more for serving

1 cup water

2 tablespoons extra virgin olive oil, plus more for cooking and serving

1 cucumber, very thinly sliced, for serving

1 avocado, sliced, for serving

Freshly ground black pepper, for serving

In a medium bowl, whisk together the chickpea flour, dill, scallions, salt, water, and the 2 tablespoons oil.

In a large nonstick skillet, heat 1 tablespoon of oil over medium-high heat. For each pancake, spoon in about 2 tablespoons of the batter and space 2 inches apart. Cook for 2 to 3 minutes, until the undersides are golden brown and the batter is just about set in the center. Flip the pancakes and cook 1 minute more, or until the pancakes are cooked through. Repeat with the remaining batter, adding more oil as necessary (you should get about 12 pancakes).

Divide the pancakes among plates and top with the cucumber and avocado. Drizzle the cucumber and avocado with a little oil and sprinkle with salt, pepper, and dill.

Cherry and Coffee Smoothie Bowl

Cherries and coffee are two of my favorite things,
so I made them colleagues.

Active: 5 min / Total: 5 min / Serves 2

½ frozen sliced banana

1½ cups frozen pitted cherries

3 tablespoons almond butter

3 to 5 tablespoons brewed coffee or
espresso

2 tablespoons hemp hearts

¼ cup dried (unsweetened) coconut
chips

Fresh fruit, such as mango and
blueberries, for serving

In a blender, combine the banana, cherries, almond butter, and
3 tablespoons of the coffee. Blend until very thick and creamy. Add a
little more coffee, if necessary.

Spoon into bowls and top with the hemp hearts, coconut chips, and
fresh fruit.

Breakfast Cookies

Cookies are an efficient breakfast. We make ours not-too-sweet and serve them deliciously warm.

Active: 10 min / Total: 25 min / Makes 12 cookies

2 tablespoons flaxseed meal

5 tablespoons water

½ cup crunchy peanut butter or almond butter

2 tablespoons pure maple syrup

1 teaspoon pure vanilla extract

¼ teaspoon kosher salt

1 cup old-fashioned rolled oats

¼ cup dried unsweetened cranberries or cherries

Heat the oven to 350°F. Line a sheet pan with parchment paper.

In a medium bowl, stir together the flaxseed meal and water. Let stand for about 10 minutes, or until slightly thickened. Whisk in the peanut butter, maple syrup, vanilla, and salt.

Add the oats and cranberries and stir to combine. Scoop the dough into heaping tablespoon–size mounds and place on the prepared pan.

Bake for 10 to 12 minutes, until set.

Overnight Oats

I love how rich in texture, flavor, and
sweetness these are by morning.
Just grab and go.

Active: 5 min / Total: 8 hrs / Each serves 1

Peanut Butter and Jelly

⅓ cup old-fashioned
rolled oats

2 teaspoons chia seeds

2 teaspoons raspberry
or strawberry jam

1 tablespoon peanut
butter

Small pinch of kosher
salt

½ cup unsweetened
plant-based milk,
such as cashew, oat,
or almond; or water

Apricot Ginger

⅓ cup old-fashioned
rolled oats

2 teaspoons chia seeds

2 teaspoons apricot
preserves

1 teaspoon grated
peeled fresh ginger

Small pinch of kosher
salt

½ cup unsweetened
plant-based milk,
such as cashew, oat,
or almond; or water

Pumpkin

⅓ cup old-fashioned
rolled oats

2 teaspoons chia seeds

1 tablespoon canned
pumpkin puree

1 teaspoon pure maple
syrup

½ teaspoon pure vanilla
extract

¼ teaspoon ground
cinnamon

¼ teaspoon grated
nutmeg

Small pinch of ground
cloves

Small pinch of kosher
salt

⅓ cup unsweetened
plant-based milk,
such as cashew, oat,
or almond; or water

Date and Coconut

⅓ cup old-fashioned
rolled oats

2 teaspoons chia seeds

1 pitted date, soaked
in hot water for 10
minutes

1 tablespoon
unsweetened
shredded coconut

Small pinch of kosher
salt

½ cup unsweetened
plant-based milk,
such as cashew, oat,
or almond; or water

For each variation, in a 6-ounce container with a tight-fitting lid, combine
the oats, chia seeds, and flavorings and stir together. Stir in the milk. Cover
tightly and refrigerate overnight (or for up to 3 days).

Stir well before serving.

French Toast

This easy recipe is a win for you. Use a nice structured loaf, with crust.

Active: 15 min / Total: 15 min / Serves 4

2 ripe bananas

2 cups unsweetened plant-based milk, such as cashew, oat, or almond

2 teaspoons pure vanilla extract

½ teaspoon ground cinnamon

Small pinch of kosher salt

1 loaf rustic bread, such as ciabatta

Coconut oil, for cooking

Pure maple syrup, for serving

Fresh fruit and berries, for serving

In a blender, combine the bananas, milk, vanilla, cinnamon, and salt. Blend until smooth and creamy. Pour into a baking dish large enough to hold 2 slices of the bread in a single layer.

From the loaf of bread, slice eight 1-inch-thick slices.

Add 2 slices of the bread to the batter and soak for 30 seconds per side.

In a large nonstick skillet, heat about 2 teaspoons of oil over medium heat. One at a time, lift out the bread slices, shake off excess batter, and add to the skillet. If your skillet is large enough, add more soaked slices of bread. Cook for 2 to 4 minutes per side, until golden brown and crisp at the edges. Repeat with the remaining bread.

Serve with warm maple syrup, fresh fruit, and berries.

Mealtime

Spaghetti and Meatless Balls

Meatballs are something you might miss in your
daily life if you are vegan all the time. These offer the same
type of experience, without the meat and dairy.
Serve on top of spaghetti. Make a hero sandwich. Eat
in salads. Versatile, filling, and tasty!

Active: 20 min / **Total: 1 hr 10 min** / **Serves 4**

1 medium eggplant (about 1¼ pounds), peeled and cut into ½-inch cubes

8 ounces medium button mushrooms, quartered

3 cloves garlic, smashed and peeled

¼ cup extra virgin olive oil

1 teaspoon kosher salt

¼ teaspoon freshly ground black pepper

¼ teaspoon crushed red pepper flakes

One 15.5-ounce can chickpeas, drained and rinsed, or 1½ cups cooked chickpeas

½ cup fresh flat-leaf parsley leaves, plus more for serving

1 teaspoon dried oregano

¾ cup panko breadcrumbs

Your favorite spaghetti with marinara recipe

Heat the oven to 425°F.

On a rimmed sheet pan, combine the eggplant, mushrooms, and garlic. Drizzle with the oil and sprinkle with ½ teaspoon of the salt, the black pepper, and the red pepper flakes. Toss to coat, then spread into a single layer. Roast for 30 to 35 minutes, stirring halfway through, until the vegetables are tender. Let cool.

Put the chickpeas, roasted vegetables, parsley, oregano, and the remaining ½ teaspoon salt in a food processor. Pulse several times until finely chopped but not completely smooth. Scoop the mixture into a medium bowl. Stir in the breadcrumbs.

Line a sheet pan with parchment paper.

Roll the mixture into about 2-tablespoon-size balls (you should get 22) and place on the prepared sheet pan.

Bake for 20 to 25 minutes, until golden brown, and crisp around the edges.

Add to the marinara sauce and serve over spaghetti. (To maintain their crisp edges, stir the meatless balls into the warmed marinara right before serving.) Sprinkle with parsley.

Roasted, Smashed Potatoes with Fixin's

This is a great vehicle for our Chipotle Cashew Queso. Though, I never turn down a chance to use ketchup.

Active: 15 min / **Total: 1 hr 15 min** / **Serves 4**

Four 6- to 8-ounce Yukon Gold or red potatoes

¾ teaspoon kosher salt, plus more for potato water

½ cup extra virgin olive oil

¼ teaspoon freshly ground black pepper

2 cups fresh baby spinach or arugula

1 recipe Chipotle Cashew Queso (page 208)

4 scallions (white and light green parts), thinly sliced

½ cup fresh cilantro leaves

First boil the potatoes: Put them in a medium saucepan and cover with cold water by 2 inches, then salt it. Place over medium-high heat and let come to a boil. Reduce the heat to a gentle simmer for 25 to 30 minutes, until the potatoes can be easily pierced to the center with a paring knife. Drain the water and pass the potatoes under cold running water so they are cool enough to handle. (This can be done the day before.)

Heat the oven to 425°F.

Now smash and roast: Drizzle 2 tablespoons of the oil on a rimmed sheet pan. Place the potatoes in the oil. Using a wide metal spatula, a plate, or the palm of your hand, gently smash the potatoes so they are about 1 inch thick but still of one piece. Drizzle them with the remaining 6 tablespoons of the oil, making sure to get the oil in the cracks. Sprinkle the tops with salt and pepper. Roast for 25 to 30 minutes, until the undersides are golden brown and crisp. Flip the potatoes and roast for 10 to 15 minutes more, until crisp all around.

Divide the potatoes among plates. Top with the spinach and a big dollop of the Chipotle Cashew Queso. Sprinkle with scallions and cilantro.

Butternut Squash and Quinoa Soup

I love all of the flavors in this soup. It's so thick and hearty you could almost call it a stew.

Active: 25 min / Total: 1 hr 15 min / Serves 4

1 butternut squash (about 2¼ pounds)

3 tablespoons plus 2 teaspoons extra virgin olive oil

1 large yellow onion, chopped

1½ teaspoons kosher salt, plus more to taste

2 medium carrots, cut into ¼-inch dice

2 ribs celery, cut into ¼-inch dice

2 cloves garlic, finely chopped

1 tablespoon grated peeled fresh ginger

2 teaspoons curry powder

5½ to 6 cups water or Vegetable Broth (page 224)

¼ teaspoon freshly ground black pepper, plus more for serving

½ cup quinoa

4 cups torn kale leaves

Heat the oven to 400°F.

Cut the butternut squash in half lengthwise. Place on a rimmed sheet pan and drizzle the flesh with the 2 teaspoons oil. Flip over so they lie cut side down. Roast for 45 to 50 minutes, until very tender.

While the squash cooks, in a large pot or Dutch oven, heat the 3 tablespoons oil over medium-high heat. Add the onion and ¼ teaspoon of the salt. Cook, stirring occasionally, for 5 to 6 minutes, until softened. Add the carrots and celery and cook, stirring often, for 7 to 8 minutes, until softened. Add the garlic, ginger, and curry powder and cook, stirring, for 1 minute. Add 5½ cups of the water and let come to a boil.

Scoop out and discard the seeds from the squash, then scoop out the flesh (you should get about 2¼ cups). Add the squash to the soup and break it up with your spoon. Add the pepper and the remaining 1¼ teaspoons salt. Once it starts to boil, stir in the quinoa. Reduce the heat to medium-low, cover tightly, and simmer, stirring occasionally, for about 15 minutes, or until the quinoa is tender. Stir in the kale and simmer for 3 to 5 minutes, until tender.

If the soup is a little thick, add the remaining ½ cup water. Taste for salt; you may want to add a little more. Serve topped with some more pepper.

Taco Salad

My kids are devoted to the Chipotle restaurant chain, and they have given this their endorsement. If you already have the "Meat" and the Pico de Gallo in the fridge, this comes together quickly.

Active: 20 min / Total: 20 min / Serves 4

1 recipe "Meat" (page 219)

8 cups shredded romaine lettuce (from about 3 hearts of romaine)

4 medium carrots, thinly sliced

1 avocado, cut into chunks

2 cups Pico de Gallo (page 221) or store-bought salsa

½ cup roasted pepitas

Tortilla chips, for serving

Divide the lettuce evenly among bowls. Top with the "Meat," carrots, avocado, Pico de Gallo, and pepitas. Serve with tortilla chips.

Sloppy Joes

Make a batch of this filling for the week. Serve it on a toasted
potato bun and you have a meal in a minute.

Active: 25 min / Total: 25 min / Serves 4

2 cloves garlic, smashed and peeled

1 medium yellow onion, cut into
1-inch chunks

1 red bell pepper, cored, seeded, and
cut into 1-inch chunks

3 tablespoons extra virgin olive oil,
plus more for the buns

1¼ teaspoons kosher salt

1 small head of cauliflower, cut or
broken into florets

One 15.5-ounce can cannellini beans,
drained and rinsed, or 1½ cups
cooked cannellini beans

6 tablespoons tomato paste

2 tablespoons apple cider vinegar

2 tablespoons dark brown sugar

2 teaspoons chili powder

¼ teaspoon freshly ground black
pepper

⅛ teaspoon cayenne pepper

½ cup water

4 hamburger potato buns

Bread and butter pickles, for
serving

Your favorite potato chips, for
serving (optional)

In a food processor, finely chop the garlic. Add the onion and bell pepper
and pulse several times until evenly (but not too finely) chopped.

In a large skillet, heat the oil over medium-high heat. Add the onion
mixture and ¼ teaspoon of the salt and cook, stirring often, for 6 to
7 minutes, until tender.

Meanwhile, place the cauliflower florets in the food processor. Pulse
several times until chopped into very small, but not fine, pieces. You'll
need 4 cups of chopped cauliflower.

Add the cauliflower to the skillet and cook, stirring often, for 5 to
6 minutes, until crisp-tender. Stir in the beans.

In a small bowl, stir together the tomato paste, vinegar, brown sugar,
chili powder, black pepper, cayenne pepper, the remaining 1 teaspoon
salt, and the water. Stir into the cauliflower mixture. Reduce the heat
to medium-low and simmer for 2 to 3 minutes, until heated through.

To heat the hamburger buns, in a large skillet heat a thin layer of oil.
Place the buns cut side down in the skillet. Cook for about 1 minute, or
until the undersides are golden brown.

Dividing evenly, spoon the mixture among the hamburger buns and top
with pickles. Serve with potato chips, if using.

Sweet and Tangy Cauliflower Lettuce Cups

This is a highly sought-after recipe on my website, so I am including it for you here. I always double this quantity, as these seem to disappear quickly.

Active: 20 min / Total: 40 min / Serves 4

For the cauliflower

1 large head of cauliflower, cut or broken into small florets

2 tablespoons extra virgin olive oil

¼ teaspoon kosher salt

3 tablespoons lower-sodium tamari or lower-sodium soy sauce

1 tablespoon unseasoned rice vinegar

1 tablespoon Sriracha, plus more if you like it spicier

1 teaspoon toasted sesame oil

1 tablespoon grated peeled fresh ginger

1 teaspoon dark brown sugar

3 tablespoons water

1½ teaspoons cornstarch

For the assembly

1 head of Boston or butter lettuce, leaves separated

1 cucumber, very thinly sliced

3 scallions (white and light green parts), thinly sliced

½ cup roasted cashews, chopped

Make the cauliflower: Heat the oven to 425°F.

Place the cauliflower florets on a rimmed sheet pan. Drizzle with the olive oil and sprinkle with the salt. Use your hands to toss, then spread into a single layer. Roast for about 30 minutes, or until golden brown and tender.

Meanwhile, in a small bowl, combine the tamari, vinegar, Sriracha, sesame oil, ginger, brown sugar, water, and cornstarch.

Once the cauliflower has finished roasting, heat the tamari mixture in a medium skillet over medium-high heat. Add the cauliflower and stir to coat. Let simmer for 1 minute, or until the sauce has thickened.

To assemble: Spread out the lettuce leaves on plates or a platter. Layer each leaf with several slices of cucumber, then spoon in the cauliflower mixture. Top with the scallions and cashews.

Tomato Soup with Sourdough Croutons

My son Shep is a tomato soup guy so, of course,
when I needed someone to tell me that "kids would eat this
even though it's vegan," he gave it a stamp of approval.

Active: 20 min / **Total: 40 min** / **Serves 4**

¼ cup extra virgin olive oil

1 large yellow onion, thinly sliced

1 teaspoon kosher salt

1 clove garlic, smashed and peeled

1 tablespoon tomato paste

One 28-ounce can whole peeled
  tomatoes

⅛ to ¼ teaspoon crushed red
  pepper flakes

¼ teaspoon freshly ground black
  pepper

2½ cups water or Vegetable Broth
  (page 224)

2 cups Homemade Croutons
  (page 223)

8 fresh chives

For the soup, in a large pot or Dutch oven, heat the oil over medium-high heat. Add the onion and ¼ teaspoon of the salt and stir to coat. Cook for 12 to 15 minutes, stirring occasionally with a wooden spoon, until the onion is very tender and beginning to caramelize. Add the garlic and cook, stirring, for 1 to 2 minutes, until fragrant. Add the tomato paste and cook, stirring, for 1 to 2 minutes to caramelize the tomato paste.

Add the tomatoes, red pepper flakes, black pepper, the remaining ¾ teaspoon salt, and the water. Let the mixture come to a boil, then reduce the heat to medium and simmer, partially covered, for 15 minutes. Break up the tomatoes with a spoon as they cook.

Using a handheld or regular blender, puree the soup until very smooth. If it's too thick, add a splash of water. Taste for salt; you might want to add a little more.

Divide the soup among bowls and top with the croutons. Using scissors, snip the chives over the tops.

Broccoli Quesadillas with Chipotle Cashew Queso

These are quick and thus made often at our house.
I like to keep the filling on hand.

Active: 15 min / **Total: 20 min** / **Serves 4**

2½ cups finely chopped raw broccoli

4 scallions (white and light green parts), chopped

¼ cup chopped fresh cilantro

¼ teaspoon kosher salt

1 cup Chipotle Cashew Queso (page 208)

Four 8-inch flour tortillas

4 teaspoons extra virgin olive oil

Hot sauce, for serving

In a medium bowl, combine the broccoli, scallions, cilantro, and salt. Add the Chipotle Cashew Queso and stir to combine with the broccoli mixture.

Lay out the tortillas. Dividing evenly, spoon the mixture onto one side of each tortilla and spread it evenly to cover just that half. Fold the tortillas in half and press together.

In a medium skillet, heat 2 teaspoons of the oil over medium heat. Add 2 of the quesadillas to the skillet and cook for 2 to 3 minutes per side, until golden brown and crisp. Repeat with the remaining 2 teaspoons oil and the quesadillas. Slice and serve with hot sauce, for dipping.

Fresh Tomato Pasta

This recipe was how I subtly lassoed Jerry
into being a vegan, at times.

Active: 15 min / Total: 25 min / Serves 4 to 6

1 teaspoon kosher salt, plus more
  for pasta water and to taste

1 pound pasta, such as fusilli

¼ cup extra virgin olive oil

4 cloves garlic, thinly sliced

1 tablespoon tomato paste

3 pints cherry or grape tomatoes

½ cup water

1 sprig fresh basil, plus more leaves
  for serving

¼ teaspoon freshly ground black
  pepper

¼ teaspoon crushed red pepper
  flakes

Small pinch of sugar

Bring a large pot of water to a boil, then salt it. Cook the pasta
according to the package directions and drain into a colander.

Meanwhile, in a large pot or Dutch oven, heat the oil over medium heat.
Add the garlic and cook, stirring, for 1 to 2 minutes, until light golden
brown. Add the tomato paste and cook, stirring, for 30 seconds.

Add the tomatoes, water, basil sprig, the 1 teaspoon salt, the black
pepper, red pepper flakes, and sugar. Cover tightly and cook, stirring
once, for 8 to 10 minutes, until the tomatoes burst. Remove the lid and
simmer for 3 to 5 minutes, until the sauce thickens slightly.

Add the pasta to the sauce and stir well to coat. Taste for seasoning;
you may want to add a little more salt.

Serve topped with basil leaves.

Quinoa Patties

The patties are great for breakfast, lunch,
or dinner. And a good reason to keep cooked quinoa
and sweet potato on hand. Here we serve them in
lettuce leaves with Sriracha Dressing.

Active: 20 min / Total: 20 min / Serves 4

2¼ cups cooked and cooled quinoa

1 cup baked and mashed sweet
potato

4 scallions (white and light green
parts), chopped, plus more for
serving

¼ cup chopped fresh cilantro or flat-
leaf parsley

½ teaspoon kosher salt, plus more
to taste

¼ teaspoon freshly ground black
pepper, plus more for serving

2 tablespoons extra virgin olive oil,
plus more if necessary

Romaine or butter lettuce leaves,
for serving

Sliced avocado, for serving

1 recipe Sriracha Dressing
(page 210)

In a large bowl, combine the quinoa, sweet potato, scallions, cilantro,
salt, and pepper. Stir together until thoroughly combined. Taste for
salt; you may want to add a pinch more.

Divide the mixture evenly into 8 portions for small patties or 4 portions
for large ones. Form into ¾-inch-thick patties, pressing together tightly
so they hold their shape.

In a large nonstick skillet, heat the 2 tablespoons oil over medium-high
heat. Add the patties and cook for 3 to 4 minutes per side, until both
sides are golden brown and crispy. (You may need to add a little more oil.)

Serve the patties in lettuce leaves and top with avocado and Sriracha
Dressing, and sprinkle with scallions and pepper.

Black Bean Burgers

A hearty burger-like experience. If you have
the energy, make your own salsa.

Active: 25 min / Total: 25 min / Serves 4

One 15.5-ounce can black beans,
drained and rinsed, or 1¾ cups
cooked black beans

¼ cup roasted, unsalted sunflower
seeds

1¼ cups cooked and cooled quinoa

½ red bell pepper, cored, seeded,
and cut into ¼-inch dice

2 scallions (white and light green
parts), thinly sliced

¼ cup chopped fresh cilantro

1½ teaspoons chili powder

½ teaspoon ground cumin

¼ teaspoon chipotle powder

½ teaspoon kosher salt

2 tablespoons extra virgin olive oil,
plus more if necessary

4 hamburger buns

Shredded romaine lettuce, for
serving

Sliced avocado, for serving

1 recipe Pico de Gallo (page 221) or
store-bought salsa, for serving

In a food processor, combine the black beans and sunflower seeds.
Pulse several times until very finely chopped but not completely
smooth. Transfer to a medium bowl. Stir in the quinoa, bell pepper,
scallions, cilantro, chili powder, cumin, chipotle powder, and salt.

Form the mixture into four ½-inch-thick patties, pressing together
tightly so they hold their shape.

In a large nonstick skillet, heat the oil over medium-high heat. Add the
patties and cook for 4 to 5 minutes, until a nice brown crust forms on
the undersides. Carefully flip and cook 4 to 5 minutes more, adding a
little more oil to the skillet, if necessary.

To heat the hamburger buns, in the skillet, heat a thin layer of oil. Place
the buns cut side down in the skillet. Cook for about 1 minute, or until
the undersides are golden brown.

Build your burgers with the buns, lettuce, avocado, Pico de Gallo, and
the black bean patties.

Roasted Chiles Rellenos

A favorite of Jerry Seinfeld; believe me, I was surprised, too.
These are so easy and quick to make.

Active: 15 min / Total: 30 min / Serves 4

4 large poblano peppers

1 red bell pepper, cored, seeded, and cut into ¼-inch dice

1 cup fresh corn (from 1 to 2 ears)

½ medium red onion, chopped

One 15.5-ounce can pinto beans, drained and rinsed, or 1½ cups cooked pinto beans

2 cups shredded plant-based cheddar cheese (We like Violife)

½ teaspoon kosher salt

¼ teaspoon freshly ground black pepper

Store-bought salsa or 1 recipe Ranchero Sauce (page 208) or Pico de Gallo (page 221), for serving

Fresh cilantro leaves, for serving

Heat the oven to 425°F.

Cut the poblanos in half lengthwise through the stem so they will lie flat and not wobble. Remove the cores and seeds but leave the stems intact. Place the poblanos in a large baking dish.

In a large bowl, combine the bell pepper, corn, onion, beans, cheddar, salt, and black pepper and toss together. Fill the poblano halves with the mixture.

Cover the dish tightly with foil. Roast for 20 to 25 minutes, until the cheese is melted and the poblanos are tender.

Serve the chiles rellenos topped with salsa and cilantro.

Reimagining Mealtime

Picture the traditional American dinner plate. What's on it? An animal protein, starch, and a veggie. Right? This image is iconic, so ingrained over time that we've convinced ourselves that it is the only satisfying meal. I still do it: even though I grew up in a household where tofu was often substituted for chicken, our plates looked like this every night.

Enter vegan food. Eating establishments like Chopt and Chipotle, by offering salads and veggie or smoothie "bowls," have, over the past decade, guided us toward more plant-based meals. Bowls are hugely popular even at my house, where my kids are hesitant about eating anything too healthy, and reimagining the plate has helped us shift our collective mindset toward a different way of thinking about mealtime.

The recipes in this book replace that established source of protein with plant foods like whole grains, nuts, beans and other legumes, and a variety of other vegetables. Your plate will look different. Before long, your body will adjust. You'll have more energy and feel healthier.

You will not see a big hunk of meat protein on your plate. Does that mean you'll starve or be undernourished? Not likely. In fact, there's a debate around just how much protein the body needs. Any number I log in this book may change with the next study (which will, in all likelihood, be sponsored by the egg, beef, or animal-based-food industry).

You can ease into veganism. It doesn't have to be all or nothing. You might worry that our Grilled Broccoli with Quinoa Salad and Lemon Tahini Dressing (page 112), Roasted Cauliflower Wedges with Ranchero Sauce (page 142), or Spice Roasted Sweet Potatoes and Chickpeas with Smoky Tahini Dressing (page 87) won't be a full meal. If you are terrified of starving, start with them as a side dish and gradually swap out that meat.

You will not starve, I promise.

It takes time to change habits. Your system needs to adapt to new, cleaner foods. It needs to learn to trust itself. My meat-loving husband and I both are in love with the satisfying fullness that comes with the meals in this book. We feel good after dinner; we no longer eat and then lie on the sofa, needing to recover from the meal. We eat vegan meals, at times, and then go for a twenty- to thirty-minute walk. That is our recipe for feeling good, catching up while our kids do homework, and enjoying a restful night's sleep.

Once your body realizes vegan food can be flavorful, filling, and very satisfying, your mind will follow. Believe me. You will not starve, I promise.

Butternut Squash Risotto

A creamy, rich, and flavorful meal for an elegant
evening or a weekend lunch.

Active: 55 min / **Total: 55 min** / **Serves 4**

1 small butternut squash (about
1½ pounds), halved lengthwise

1 teaspoon plus 3 tablespoons extra
virgin olive oil

4 cups water or Vegetable Broth
(page 224)

1 large yellow onion, chopped

1 teaspoon kosher salt, plus more to
taste

1 clove garlic, finely chopped

1¼ cups arborio rice

½ cup dry white wine, such as pinot
grigio

1 teaspoon chopped fresh oregano,
plus more for serving

¼ teaspoon crushed red pepper
flakes

¼ teaspoon freshly ground black
pepper, plus more for serving

Nutritional yeast, for serving
(optional)

Heat the oven to 400°F.

Rub the flesh of one half of the squash with the 1 teaspoon oil (reserve
the other squash half for another use). Place the squash cut side down
on a sheet pan and roast 40 to 45 minutes, until very tender. Scoop out
the seeds and discard. Scoop out the flesh and measure 1 cup.

While the squash roasts, in a medium saucepan, heat the water over
low heat to keep warm while you cook.

In a large skillet, heat the 3 tablespoons oil over medium-high heat.
Add the onion and ¼ teaspoon of the salt. Cook, stirring occasionally,
for 7 to 8 minutes, until tender. Add the garlic and cook, stirring, for 30
seconds, or until fragrant. Add the rice and cook, stirring, for 1 minute.
Add the wine and stir until it's nearly evaporated.

Reduce the heat to medium-low. Add 1 cup of the warm water, the
oregano, red pepper flakes, black pepper, and the remaining ¾ teaspoon
salt. Let simmer gently, stirring often, until the water is absorbed.

Add 2 more cups of the warm water to the rice, and while it simmers,
stir occasionally, until the water is absorbed.

Stir the squash into the rice until it's well incorporated.

Now add just ½ cup of the warm water to the rice and stir until it's
nearly absorbed. Taste the rice for doneness; it should be tender but
still a little chewy in the middle. If it's too firm, stir in the remaining
½ warm cup water and let it cook a little longer. Remove from the heat
when the rice is done. The risotto should be a little loose, not stiff. You
can add a splash of water, if necessary, to loosen it. Taste for salt; you
may want to add a pinch more.

Serve the risotto topped with some more oregano, black pepper, and a
sprinkle of nutritional yeast, if using.

Old-School Salad

This is our version of a "growing up in the '70s pizza parlor salad."

Active: 20 min / Total: 20 min / Serves 4

8 cups chopped romaine lettuce
(from about 3 hearts of romaine)

1 red bell pepper, cored, seeded, and
thinly sliced into strips

1 cucumber, thinly sliced into rounds

1 small red onion, very thinly sliced

12 medium button mushrooms,
wiped clean and thinly sliced

1 recipe House Vinaigrette
(page 215)

1 recipe Homemade
Croutons (page 223)

Freshly ground black
pepper, for serving

Put the lettuce in a large shallow serving bowl. Scatter the bell pepper, cucumber, onion, and mushrooms over the lettuce. Drizzle on as much of the vinaigrette as you like. Top with the croutons. Sprinkle with black pepper.

Sweet Potato and Cauliflower Fritters

It is impossible to stop eating these. You can chop the cauliflower and grate the sweet potato by hand or use a food processor.

Active: 25 min / **Total: 25 min** / **Makes about 12 fritters**

2 cups chopped cauliflower

2 cups grated sweet potato

4 scallions (white and light green parts), chopped

3 tablespoons chopped fresh cilantro or flat-leaf parsley

1 cup all-purpose flour, spooned and leveled

1½ teaspoons ground cumin

¾ teaspoon kosher salt, plus more for serving

¼ teaspoon freshly ground black pepper

⅛ teaspoon cayenne pepper

6 tablespoons water

Extra virgin olive oil, for frying

1 lemon, cut into wedges

In a large bowl, stir together the cauliflower, sweet potato, scallions, cilantro, flour, cumin, salt, black pepper, and cayenne pepper. Add the water and stir well to combine. The batter should be stiff and hold together.

In a large nonstick skillet, heat about ⅛ inch of oil over medium-high heat. For each fritter, scoop in a dollop of batter and flatten and press together a little with the back of your spoon so the fritter is about 2 inches wide and ½ inch thick. Space the fritters about 1 inch apart in the skillet. Cook for 3 to 4 minutes per side, until golden brown and crisp. Transfer to a paper towel–lined plate. Cook the remaining fritters, adding more oil as necessary.

Sprinkle the fritters with a little salt and serve with lemon wedges.

Sweet Potato and Cauliflower
Fritters, page 65

Moroccan Spiced Chickpea Stew

Borrowing from Morocco here with this spice combo.
You may want to save the liquid from the chickpeas
(aquafaba) to make Eggplant Cutlets (page 115) or Whipped
"Cream" for your Strawberry Pie (page 190).

Active: 25 min / Total: 50 min / Serves 4

3 tablespoons extra virgin olive oil

1 large yellow onion, thinly sliced

1 teaspoon kosher salt, plus more to taste

1 clove garlic, finely chopped

2 teaspoons ground cumin

1 teaspoon paprika

½ teaspoon ground cinnamon

1 tablespoon tomato paste

One 14.5-ounce can diced tomatoes

1 red bell pepper, cored, seeded, and sliced

3 medium carrots, cut into 3-inch sticks

Two 15.5-ounce cans chickpeas, drained and rinsed, or 3 cups cooked chickpeas

2 cups water

¼ teaspoon freshly ground black pepper

⅛ teaspoon cayenne pepper

1 lemon

1 cup couscous

½ cup golden raisins

¼ cup chopped fresh cilantro or flat-leaf parsley, for serving

In a large pot or Dutch oven, heat the oil over medium-high heat. Add the onion and ¼ teaspoon of the salt. Cook, stirring occasionally, for 8 to 10 minutes, until very tender. Add the garlic, cumin, paprika, and cinnamon and cook, stirring and scraping the bottom of the pot with a wooden spoon, for 1 minute, until fragrant. Add the tomato paste and cook, stirring, for 1 minute.

Add the tomatoes, bell pepper, carrots, chickpeas, water, black pepper, cayenne pepper, and the remaining ¾ teaspoon salt. Using a vegetable peeler, peel 3 wide strips of the lemon peel and add to the pot (reserve the lemon for another use). Let it come to a boil, then reduce the heat so it simmers gently. Cover tightly and simmer for about 25 minutes, or until the carrots are tender.

While the stew cooks, prepare the couscous according to the package directions.

Stir the raisins into the stew. Remove the pot from the heat and let it stand, partially covered, for 5 minutes. Taste for salt; you may want to add a little more.

Serve the stew with the couscous and sprinkle with cilantro.

Mexican-Style Grilled Street Corn

Slathered in spicy queso, this grilled corn
is the star of my summer meal. My kids go wild for
this, having no idea it is vegan.

Active: 10 min / Total: 20 min / Serves 4

4 ears fresh corn,
shucked

1 teaspoon extra virgin
olive oil

1 recipe Chipotle
Cashew Queso (page
208)

3 scallions (white and
light green parts),
very thinly sliced

½ cup chopped fresh
cilantro

1 lime, cut into wedges

Heat the grill to medium-high.

Lightly coat each ear of corn with
the oil. Place the corn on the grill
and grill for 10 to 12 minutes, turning
occasionally, until some of the
kernels are charred.

Spread as much of the Chipotle
Cashew Queso as you like over the
corn and sprinkle with the scallions
and cilantro. Serve with lime wedges.

Loaded Sweet Potato Fries

This is a favorite. You can make or buy the accoutrements.

Active: 25 min / Total: 45 min / Serves 4

4 medium sweet potatoes (about 2¼ pounds), peeled

3 tablespoons extra virgin olive oil

¼ teaspoon kosher salt

1½ cups "Meat" (page 219)

1½ cups shredded plant-based cheddar cheese (We like Violife)

1 recipe Guacamole (page 218) or store-bought, for serving

1 recipe Pico de Gallo (page 221) or store-bought salsa, for serving

Heat the oven to 425°F.

Cut the sweet potatoes into ½-inch-thick wedges and put them on a rimmed sheet pan. Drizzle with the oil, sprinkle with salt, and toss to coat. Arrange in a single layer and roast for 25 to 30 minutes, until the undersides are golden brown. Flip them and roast for 5 to 10 minutes more, until tender.

Crumble the "Meat" over the sweet potatoes and sprinkle with the cheese. Roast for about 5 minutes more, or until the cheese has melted.

Divide the loaded sweet potatoes among plates and top with Guacamole and Pico de Gallo.

Grilled Vegetable Skewers with Coconut Rice and Ginger-Scallion Relish

My mom taught me you can skewer and grill anything, anytime. In the deep snow—no problem, she's out there. This recipe works year-round.

Active: 45 min / Total: 45 min / Serves 4

For the skewers

4 bell peppers (any color), cored, seeded, and cut into 1-inch pieces

2 medium red onions, cut into 1-inch wedges

16 small-medium button mushrooms

3 medium zucchini, cut into 1-inch-thick rounds

3 tablespoons extra virgin olive oil

½ teaspoon kosher salt

¼ teaspoon freshly ground black pepper

For the coconut rice

1 cup water

¾ cup coconut milk

½ teaspoon kosher salt

1 cup jasmine rice

1 recipe Ginger-Scallion Relish (page 215)

Make the skewers: Heat the grill to medium-high.

Thread eight 10-inch skewers with the vegetables, dividing them as you wish. Place them on a rimmed sheet pan. Drizzle with the oil and sprinkle with salt and pepper. Roll them around to coat. (If the skewers are wooden, wrap the ends with foil to prevent burning.)

Make the rice: In a small saucepan, combine the water, coconut milk, salt, and rice and place over medium-high heat. Let come to a boil, stir once, cover tightly, and reduce the heat to low. Cook for 18 minutes, or until the liquid is absorbed and the rice is tender. Remove from the heat, fluff with a fork, and let stand, covered, for 5 minutes more.

While the rice is cooking, grill the skewers, turning them occasionally, for about 15 minutes, or until the vegetables are charred and tender.

Serve the skewers over the rice and top with the Ginger-Scallion Relish.

Vegetable Spring Rolls with Peanut Butter Dipping Sauce

These will make you feel fresh and clean from
the inside out. Dip them in the spicy and sweet dipping sauce
and the experience is complete. I know that spring rolls
can be intimidating if you haven't made them before.
I promise once you get the feel for the rice paper, you won't
want to stop rolling.

Active: 35 min / Total: 35 min / **Makes 10 spring rolls**

1 red bell pepper, cored, seeded, and
    thinly sliced

1 cucumber, sliced into 3-inch-long
    thin strips

1 cup grated carrots

¼ cup chopped fresh cilantro

3 scallions (white and light green
    parts), chopped

1 teaspoon lower-sodium tamari or
    lower-sodium soy sauce

1 teaspoon toasted sesame oil

1 teaspoon unseasoned rice vinegar

Ten 22-cm round rice paper
    wrappers

1 recipe Peanut Butter Dipping
    Sauce (page 218)

For the spring rolls, in a large bowl, combine the bell pepper, cucumber, carrots, cilantro, and scallions.

In a small bowl, stir together the tamari, oil, and vinegar. Drizzle over the vegetables and toss to coat.

Fill a large bowl or large skillet with very hot water. One at a time, dip a rice paper wrapper into the water until it just starts to soften (this should take 15 to 30 seconds). Shake off excess water. Lay the wrapper on a smooth work surface.

In the middle of the wrapper place a small, tightly packed pile of vegetables, laying them in the same direction. Roll up like a burrito: fold the ends over, then tightly roll up. Repeat with the remaining wrappers and vegetables. Serve with the Peanut Butter Dipping Sauce.

Red Curry with Zucchini Noodles

You can make the noodles with zucchini or pasta—
the sauce is what will make your head spin.

Active: 30 min / Total: 40 min / Serves 4

2-inch piece of fresh ginger, peeled and sliced

2 cloves garlic, smashed and peeled

1 jalapeño, halved (and seeded if you don't like heat)

3 tablespoons extra virgin olive oil

4 teaspoons curry powder

1 tablespoon ground coriander

¼ cup tomato paste

One 13.5-ounce can unsweetened coconut milk

1 cup water

1 teaspoon kosher salt, plus more to taste

½ teaspoon sugar

2 cups 2-inch pieces fresh green beans

2 large zucchini, spiralized on the thinnest noodle blade (about 6 cups)

3 scallions (white and light green parts), thinly sliced

Fresh cilantro leaves, for serving

2 limes, cut into wedges

In a food processor, pulse together the ginger, garlic, jalapeño, and oil into a paste.

Place the curry powder, coriander, tomato paste, coconut milk, water, and ginger paste by the stove.

Place a large saucepan over medium heat. Add the ginger paste and cook, stirring with a wooden spoon, for 1 minute, or until fragrant. Add the curry powder and coriander and cook, stirring, for 30 seconds. Now add the tomato paste and cook, stirring and scraping the bottom of the pan, for 1 to 2 minutes to caramelize the tomato paste.

Whisk in the coconut milk. Then add the water, salt, and sugar. Let it come to a simmer, then cook the curry for 3 to 4 minutes to let the flavors come together.

Add the green beans to the curry and simmer for 10 to 15 minutes, until the green beans are tender. Taste for salt; you may want to add a little more.

Divide the zucchini noodles among bowls and ladle in the curry. Top with the scallions, lots of cilantro, and a squeeze of lime.

Cauliflower Rice and Beans

This is a slightly healthier version of
rice and beans, in less time.

Active: 25 min / Total: 25 min / Serves 4

For the beans

2 tablespoons extra virgin olive oil

1 medium yellow onion, finely
chopped

½ teaspoon kosher salt

1 teaspoon ground cumin

Two 15.5-ounce cans black beans,
drained and rinsed, or 3½ cups
cooked black beans

A few shakes of your favorite hot
sauce (optional)

⅓ cup water

For the cauliflower rice

1 medium-large head of cauliflower,
cut or broken into florets

3 tablespoons extra virgin olive oil

1 teaspoon chili powder

½ teaspoon kosher salt

1 avocado, sliced, for serving

1 recipe Pico de Gallo (page 221) or
store-bought salsa, for serving

Make the beans: In a medium saucepan, heat the oil over medium-high heat. Add the onion and salt and cook for 8 to 10 minutes, stirring often, until very tender. Add the cumin and cook, stirring, for 30 seconds. Add the beans, hot sauce, and water. Reduce the heat to low and simmer for 5 minutes, or until heated through.

Make the cauliflower rice: Add half of the florets to a food processor. Pulse several times until chopped (fine but not too fine). Transfer to a bowl and repeat with the remaining cauliflower (you should get about 5½ cups).

In a large skillet, heat the oil over medium-high heat. Add the cauliflower and cook for 5 to 6 minutes, stirring often, until the rawness from the cauliflower cooks out (but you still want it to be al dente, not completely soft). Stir in the chili powder and salt.

Divide the beans and rice among bowls. Top with the avocado and Pico de Gallo.

Grilled Portobello Burgers

Skeptics will say this is "not a burger." So what. Do it your way.

Active: 20 min / Total: 35 min / Serves 4

4 large portobello mushrooms

½ cup extra virgin olive oil, plus more for the onion

¼ cup fresh lemon juice

2 cloves garlic, grated or finely chopped

2 teaspoons chopped fresh rosemary

1 red onion, sliced into ¼-inch-thick rounds

¾ teaspoon kosher salt

⅛ teaspoon plus ¼ teaspoon freshly ground black pepper

1 head of iceberg lettuce

1 recipe Ranch Dressing (page 214)

Remove the stems from the mushrooms and discard. Using a damp paper towel, wipe the mushroom caps clean.

In a large baking dish, stir together the oil, lemon juice, garlic, and rosemary. Add the mushrooms and coat them with the marinade. Let marinate for 15 minutes.

Heat the grill to medium-high.

Lightly coat the onion with a little oil and sprinkle with ¼ teaspoon of the salt and the ⅛ teaspoon pepper.

Sprinkle the mushrooms with the remaining ½ teaspoon salt and the ¼ teaspoon pepper. Grill the mushrooms and onion for 4 to 5 minutes per side, until tender. Alternatively, you can cook the mushrooms and onion in a cast-iron skillet for the same amount of time.

Cut the head of lettuce in half, then tear off a stack of leaves to make a bed on each of four plates. Top with a mushroom, onion slices, and a spoonful of Ranch Dressing.

Potato and Caramelized Onion Tart

Perfect fare for a lovely brunch. Serve this with salad greens dressed in House Vinaigrette (page 215). If you want to be organized on the day of, the dough and caramelized onions can be made ahead of time.

Active: 50 min / Total: 2 hrs / Serves 4

For the crust

2 cups all-purpose flour, spooned and leveled, plus more for rolling

¾ teaspoon kosher salt

⅓ cup extra virgin olive oil

5 to 6 tablespoons water

For the topping

¼ cup plus 1 tablespoon extra virgin olive oil

2 large yellow onions, thinly sliced with the grain (from top to stem)

¾ teaspoon kosher salt

Three 4-ounce Yukon Gold potatoes, scrubbed

⅛ teaspoon freshly ground black pepper

Chopped fresh dill, for serving

Make the crust: In a large bowl, whisk together the flour and salt. Add the oil. Use a fork or your fingertips to incorporate the oil until coarse crumbs form. Add 5 tablespoons of the water and stir in with a fork. The dough should look a little shaggy and just start to come together into one piece. Add the remaining tablespoon of water, if necessary. Shape into a 1-inch-thick disk, wrap tightly, and let rest on the counter for at least 45 minutes. The longer it rests, the easier it will be to roll out.

While the dough rests, make the topping: In a large pot or Dutch oven, heat the ¼ cup oil over medium heat. Add the onions and stir to coat with the oil. Stir in ½ teaspoon of the salt. Cover tightly and cook for 10 minutes, stirring once. Remove the lid and continue to cook, stirring and scraping the bottom of the pot occasionally with a wooden spoon, for about 30 minutes more, until caramelized to a deep golden brown and very soft (reduce the heat if the onions start to scorch). Remove from the heat and let cool.

Heat the oven to 400°F.

Continues

Potato and Caramelized Onion Tart

CONTINUED

On a large piece of parchment paper, roll out the dough to a circle about 12 inches in diameter and ¼ inch thick (the dough is sturdy, so you don't have to be too delicate with it). Sprinkle with a little flour both on top and underneath as you roll, to prevent sticking. Slide the parchment and dough onto a large rimmed sheet pan.

Spread the onions evenly over the dough, leaving a 1-inch border. Fold the border over the edge of the onions.

Using a sharp knife or mandoline, slice the potatoes into very thin rounds (about 1/16 inch thick). Starting from the outside, just over the inside edge of the crust, lay the potatoes in concentric circles and work your way to the center, overlapping as you go. Brush the potatoes with the 1 tablespoon oil. Sprinkle with the pepper and the remaining ¼ teaspoon salt.

Bake for 45 to 55 minutes, until the crust is golden brown and the potatoes are tender and browned around the edges. Serve hot or at room temperature. Sprinkle with some dill before serving.

Spice Roasted Sweet Potatoes and Chickpeas with Smoky Tahini Dressing

Sweet potatoes are affordable, available year-round, and easy to store. You can pull this meal together easily with the rest of these pantry-friendly ingredients.

Active: 25 min / Total: 40 min / Serves 4

1¼ pounds sweet potatoes, cut into ½-inch dice

One 15.5-ounce can chickpeas, drained and rinsed, or 1½ cups cooked chickpeas

3 tablespoons extra virgin olive oil

1 teaspoon ground cumin

½ teaspoon ground coriander

½ teaspoon plus ⅛ teaspoon kosher salt

¼ teaspoon freshly ground black pepper

⅛ teaspoon cayenne pepper

1½ cups water

1 cup basmati rice

⅓ cup chopped fresh cilantro, dill, or flat-leaf parsley (or a mix)

2 scallions (white and light green parts), thinly sliced

1 recipe Smoky Tahini Dressing (page 210)

Heat the oven to 425°F.

On a rimmed sheet pan, combine the sweet potatoes, chickpeas, and oil. Toss to coat.

In a small bowl, combine the cumin, coriander, the ½ teaspoon salt, the black pepper, and the cayenne pepper. Sprinkle over the sweet potatoes and chickpeas, then toss one more time and arrange in a single layer. Roast for 25 to 30 minutes, until the sweet potato pieces are tender and golden brown.

Meanwhile, bring the water and the ⅛ teaspoon salt to a boil. Stir in the rice. Cover tightly and reduce the heat to low. Cook for 15 minutes. Remove from the heat, fluff with a fork, and let stand, covered, for 5 minutes more.

Spoon the rice onto a large serving plate. Add the sweet potatoes and chickpeas. Sprinkle the cilantro and scallions over the top and drizzle with as much of the Smoky Tahini Dressing as you like.

Roasted Garlic Pesto Pasta Salad

Gosh, it is so special when the whole family is happy with a meal. This one wins at our house every time.

Active: 15 min / Total: 25 min / Serves 4 to 6

Kosher salt for pasta water, plus more to taste

1 pound short pasta, such as gemelli

1 pint cherry tomatoes

1 recipe Roasted Garlic Pesto (page 216)

Fresh basil leaves, for serving

Bring a large pot of water to a boil, then salt it. Add the pasta and cook according to the package directions. Drain the pasta and pass under cold running water to stop the cooking and to cool. Shake out excess water and transfer to a large serving bowl.

While the pasta cooks, cut the tomatoes in half or (if large) into quarters.

Spoon the Roasted Garlic Pesto over the pasta and stir well. Taste for salt; you may want to add a little more. Serve topped with the tomatoes and several basil leaves.

Stewy White Beans

A very meaty experience, just without the meat.
You'll be rewarded grandly for taking the time to cook up
dried beans and make your own toasty croutons.

Active: 40 min / Total: 40 min (plus cooking time for beans) / Serves 4

3½ cups cooked cannellini or Great Northern beans (from 8 ounces or about 1¼ cups dried beans)

¼ cup extra virgin olive oil, plus more for serving

1 large yellow onion, chopped

½ teaspoon kosher salt, plus more to taste

3 medium carrots, cut into ¼-inch dice

2 ribs celery, cut into ¼-inch dice

1 clove garlic, chopped

1 teaspoon chopped fresh rosemary

¼ teaspoon crushed red pepper flakes

⅛ teaspoon freshly ground black pepper

3 tablespoons chopped fresh flat-leaf parsley

1 cup Homemade Croutons (page 223)

Follow the instructions for cooking dried beans on page 226. Be sure to reserve the cooking liquid.

While the beans cook, cook the vegetables. In a large pot or Dutch oven, heat the oil over medium-high heat. Add the onion and ¼ teaspoon of the salt and cook, stirring often, for 7 to 8 minutes, until tender. Add the carrots and celery and cook, stirring occasionally, for 12 to 15 minutes, until they begin to caramelize (if they start to scorch, reduce the heat to medium). Add the garlic, rosemary, red pepper flakes, black pepper, and the remaining ¼ teaspoon salt. Cook, stirring, for 1 to 2 minutes, until fragrant. Remove from the heat.

Once the beans are tender, use a strainer to scoop out the beans and add them to the vegetables.

Add 1 cup of the cooking liquid to the vegetables and stir to combine. Simmer over low heat for a few minutes to allow the liquid to thicken. Taste for salt; you may want to add a little more. If you want the beans a little stewier, add another ½ cup of the cooking liquid.

Divide the beans among bowls. Sprinkle with parsley and drizzle with a little more oil. Crumble the croutons into small pieces over the beans.

Macaroni and Cheese

I have served this many times to non-vegans and
they always go for seconds. I use cashew or almond milk
for their mild flavor, but you can always experiment
with other plant-based milks.

Active: 35 min / Total: 55 min / Serves 6

For the macaroni and cheese

½ teaspoon kosher salt, plus more
    for pasta water

1 pound short pasta, such as
    cavatappi, elbows, or small shells

3 tablespoons extra virgin olive oil

5 tablespoons all-purpose flour

4½ cups unsweetened cashew or
    almond milk

16 ounces (4 cups) shredded plant-
    based cheddar cheese (We like
    Violife)

2 tablespoons nutritional yeast

1 teaspoon dry mustard

¼ teaspoon freshly ground black
    pepper

⅛ teaspoon cayenne pepper

For the breadcrumb topping

1 cup panko or coarse dried
    breadcrumbs

3 tablespoons extra virgin olive oil

¼ teaspoon kosher salt

⅛ teaspoon freshly ground black
    pepper

1 clove garlic

2 tablespoons chopped fresh flat-
    leaf parsley, for serving

Position the oven rack about 8 inches from the top and heat the oven to
400°F.

Make the macaroni and cheese: Bring a large pot of water to a boil,
then salt it. Add the pasta and cook until it's a few minutes short of
al dente (it will continue to cook in the oven). Drain into a colander
and pass under cold running water to stop the cooking. Shake out any
excess water.

Meanwhile, to make the cheese sauce, in a large pot or Dutch oven,
heat the oil over medium heat. Add the flour and cook, stirring with
a wooden spoon, for about 3 minutes to cook out the raw flavor of the
flour. Add 1 cup of the milk and whisk until it forms a smooth paste.
Continue to whisk in the remaining milk a little at a time, at first, to
avoid lumps. Let the mixture reach a simmer while whisking often,
paying attention to the corners where the flour can collect.

Remove from the heat and add the cheese, nutritional yeast, dry
mustard, the ½ teaspoon salt, the black pepper, and the cayenne
pepper. Whisk until creamy and smooth. Add the pasta and stir well
to coat. Taste for salt; you may want to add a little more. Scrape the
mixture into a 9 x 13-inch baking dish.

Make the breadcrumb topping: In a small bowl stir together the
breadcrumbs, oil, salt, and pepper. Grate in the garlic and stir to
combine.

Sprinkle the breadcrumbs over the macaroni and cheese. Bake for
about 15 minutes, or until the sauce is bubbling. Then turn on the
broiler and broil for 1 to 3 minutes, until the breadcrumbs are golden
brown. Let cool for 5 minutes before serving and sprinkle the top with
the parsley.

Kale Quinoa Salad with Sriracha Dressing

This is my go-to lunch, served with lots
of this creamy dressing.

Active: 20 min / Total: 20 min / Serves 4

1 bunch of kale, torn into bite-size
   pieces (about 10 cups)

3 cups cooked and cooled quinoa
   or farro

1 cucumber, very thinly sliced

1 red bell pepper, cored, seeded, and
   thinly sliced

½ red onion, thinly sliced

One 15.5-ounce can chickpeas,
   drained and rinsed, or 1½ cups
   cooked chickpeas

¼ cup roasted sunflower seeds

1 recipe Sriracha Dressing
   (page 210)

Divide the kale, quinoa, cucumber, bell pepper, onion, chickpeas, and sunflower seeds among bowls.

Spoon as much of the Sriracha Dressing as you like over each salad.

Buffalo Cauliflower

Another top pick on my website. I suggest doubling this recipe because you won't have enough, trust me. The rice flour makes the cauliflower extra crispy.

Active: 25 min / Total: 25 min / Serves 4

1½ cups brown or white rice flour, spooned and leveled

⅔ cup tapioca flour, spooned and leveled

1 teaspoon kosher salt

¼ teaspoon freshly ground black pepper

1¼ cups cold water, plus more if necessary

1 large head of cauliflower, cut or broken into small florets

Extra virgin olive oil, for frying

One 12-ounce jar vegan Buffalo wing sauce

1 recipe Ranch Dressing (page 214)

Celery sticks, for serving

In a large bowl, whisk together the rice flour, tapioca flour, salt, and pepper. Whisk in the water until smooth. The mixture should have the thickness of pancake batter. If it's too thick, add a little more water. Add the cauliflower florets to the batter and stir to coat.

Line a large plate with paper towels.

In a medium saucepan, pour in about ¾ inch of oil. Heat the pan over medium until hot. You can test the heat of the oil with a drop of the batter; it should sizzle immediately.

You're going to fry the cauliflower in batches. Using tongs, lift one floret at a time out of the batter and lower it into the oil. Do not overcrowd. Fry the cauliflower for 4 to 6 minutes, turning occasionally, until crisp and golden brown at the edges. Using the tongs again, lift out each floret onto the paper towel–lined plate. Cook the remaining cauliflower.

In a large skillet, heat the Buffalo wing sauce over medium heat.

Toss the fried cauliflower in the Buffalo wing sauce and serve immediately with the Ranch Dressing and celery sticks.

Creamy Polenta with Roasted Mushrooms and Tomatoes

Rich, filling, and satisfying, this will prove to
anyone that vegan meals won't leave you hungry and sad.
While the tomatoes and mushrooms roast, cook the polenta.
Everything should be ready at the same time.

Active: 25 min / Total: 40 min / Serves 4

1½ pints cherry or grape tomatoes

1 pound medium button mushrooms, quartered

3 cloves garlic, smashed and peeled

8 sprigs fresh thyme

4 tablespoons extra virgin olive oil

1½ teaspoons kosher salt

¼ teaspoon freshly ground black pepper

½ cup dry white wine, such as pinot grigio

4 cups water

1 cup polenta (coarsely ground cornmeal)

1 tablespoon nutritional yeast (optional)

Heat the oven to 425°F.

On a rimmed sheet pan, combine the tomatoes, mushrooms, garlic, and thyme. Drizzle with 3 tablespoons of the oil and sprinkle with ½ teaspoon of the salt and the pepper. Use your hands to toss the mixture until evenly coated, then spread into a single layer. Roast for 25 to 30 minutes, or until the tomatoes start to burst and the mushrooms are tender. Pour in the wine and roast for 2 to 3 minutes more, until bubbling.

Meanwhile, in a medium saucepan, bring the water to a boil over medium-high heat. While whisking, gradually pour in the polenta. Reduce the heat to low so the polenta simmers gently. Cook for 25 to 30 minutes, stirring often with a whisk or wooden spoon, until the polenta is tender and creamy. Add the remaining 1 teaspoon salt and stir in the remaining 1 tablespoon oil. Stir in the nutritional yeast, if using.

Divide the polenta among bowls and top with the roasted tomato and mushroom mixture and any sauce that remains in the pan.

Spaghetti with Olive Oil, Garlic, and Chickpeas

Just when you think you have nothing in the house,
you can pull this off.

Active: 15 min / Total: 25 min / Serves 4 to 6

¾ teaspoon kosher salt, plus more for pasta water and to taste

1 pound pasta, such as thin spaghetti

6 tablespoons extra virgin olive oil

3 cloves garlic, finely chopped

¼ teaspoon crushed red pepper flakes

One 15.5-ounce can chickpeas, drained and rinsed, or 1½ cups cooked chickpeas

8 cups fresh baby spinach

¼ teaspoon freshly ground black pepper, plus more for serving

Nutritional yeast, for serving (optional)

Bring a large pot of water to a boil, then salt it. Cook the pasta according to the package directions. Right before you drain the pasta, reserve 1 cup of the pasta water.

Once you drain the pasta, wipe the pot dry and return it to medium heat. Add 4 tablespoons of the oil to the pot, then add the garlic and red pepper flakes. Cook, stirring, for about 30 seconds, or until the garlic is fragrant; do not let it brown. Add the reserved pasta water and the chickpeas and let simmer for 1 minute.

Add the pasta to the pot and stir to coat. Remove from the heat. Add the spinach, salt, and black pepper. Stir until the spinach wilts. Drizzle in the remaining 2 tablespoons oil and stir once more. Taste for salt; you may want to add a little more.

Serve the pasta topped with black pepper and a sprinkle of nutritional yeast, if you like.

Italian White Bean and Farro Soup

Make a batch of this tasty, pantry-friendly,
and cozy soup on a Sunday and you can put it in the
fridge or freezer for another day.

Active: 30 min / **Total: 55 min** / **Serves 4**

---

3 tablespoons extra virgin olive oil

1 large yellow onion, chopped

1½ teaspoons kosher salt, plus more
   to taste

4 medium carrots, cut into ¼-inch-
   thick half-moons

3 ribs celery, cut into ¼-inch pieces

2 cloves garlic, finely chopped

One 14-ounce can chopped or diced
   tomatoes

5 cups water or Vegetable Broth
   (page 224)

½ cup farro

2 teaspoons chopped fresh
   rosemary

¼ teaspoon freshly ground black
   pepper, plus more for serving

¼ teaspoon crushed red pepper
   flakes

4 cups spinach leaves

One 15.5-ounce can cannellini beans,
   drained and rinsed, or 1½ cups
   cooked cannellini beans

In a large pot or Dutch oven, heat the oil over medium-high heat. Add the onion and ¼ teaspoon of the salt. Cook, stirring occasionally, for 5 to 6 minutes, until softened. Add the carrots and celery and cook, stirring often, for 5 to 6 minutes, until beginning to soften. Add the garlic and cook, stirring, for about 2 minutes, or until fragrant. Add the tomatoes and cook, stirring, for 2 minutes.

Add the water, farro, rosemary, black pepper, red pepper flakes, and the remaining 1¼ teaspoons salt and let come to a boil. Reduce the heat to a simmer, cover partially with a lid, and cook for about 25 minutes, until the farro is tender.

Remove the lid and stir in the spinach and beans. Simmer for 2 to 3 minutes, until the spinach is wilted and the beans are heated through. Taste for salt; you may want to add a little more.

Divide among bowls and serve topped with a little more black pepper.

Really, You're a Vegan Now?

Life's a lot easier when everyone in a household agrees on food. In my house, that is not and has never been the case.

I quietly strategized about getting my family to eat anything vegan. Any experienced parent knows this is how you get your family to do things. You don't make bold statements and ambush people. Those who have cooked from the recipes in *Deceptively Delicious* know exactly what I mean: I made my family's favorite foods healthier by adding (as in, sneaking in) vegetables. I took the same approach with vegan food. Slowly I took out the cheese and other dairy. When I can, I use vegan cheese, and I mostly use nondairy milks when I cook.

Creating good eating habits presents challenges along the way. When my kids heard me talking about vegan meals, they started to worry. "Great, more seeds in our food," my daughter moaned. Was I going to force them to eat it, too? Of course not! Forcing kids to eat healthfully is a surefire way to get them downing Cocoa Puffs in their closets. I used the same approach for them as I did for myself: no must-haves and don't-haves. Be flexible and nonjudgmental, and don't tell yourself you're never going to eat a hamburger again.

When I started on my own vegan path, I was cooking for one. Jerry started to observe my simpler meals and would look at my colorful, cozy plate and ask, "What are you eating?"

I was a novice. I began with muesli cereal and dairy-free milk for breakfast and sweet potatoes for dinner. (Actually, they are still a satisfying and soothing meal, easy and uncomplicated. Sweet potatoes in particular are a strong lead-in to the vegan lifestyle.) Instead of sautéing greens in butter, I'd use olive oil, and lots of salt and pepper. I quickly grew to prefer them that way. My plate started to look bright and beautiful every meal. One night, after a very filling steak dinner, Jerry yelled, "Okay, I'm in!" from the sofa.

I started to make vegan desserts and pastas. Those recipes were easy sell-ins, and made my family believe. My desserts tasted deliciously "normal" and the pasta meals did, too.

I knew they wouldn't automatically dive into a bowl of grains and vegetables. I had to make foods they like. I started with the Macaroni and Cheese (page 92) and that was a huge hit. Next came the Fresh Tomato Pasta on page 52. And for dessert, the Peanut Butter Bars on page 204 and the Chocolate Sheet Cake on page 186 are always devoured.

As a result, I liberated my whole family to enjoy what I am eating, meatless, dairy-less, or not. With that modest beginning, I opened a new chapter for the Seinfeld family.

When my kids heard me talking about vegan meals, they started to worry. "Great, more seeds in our food," my daughter moaned.

Indian Spiced Lentils and Rice

The star of this winner is garam masala:
a spice blend of cardamom, cinnamon, cloves, cumin,
black pepper, and coriander.

Active: 45 min / **Total: 45 min** / **Serves 4**

¼ cup extra virgin olive oil

1 large yellow onion, thinly sliced

1⅛ teaspoons kosher salt, plus more if necessary

3 cloves garlic, smashed and peeled

2 tablespoons grated peeled fresh ginger

1 teaspoon ground cumin

1 teaspoon garam masala

One 14-ounce can whole or diced tomatoes

2½ cups water, plus more if necessary

⅛ teaspoon cayenne pepper

¼ teaspoon freshly ground black pepper

1 cup French green lentils, rinsed

1 cup basmati rice, for serving

Chopped fresh dill, for serving

1 lime, cut into wedges

In a large saucepan, heat the oil over medium-high heat. Add the onion and ¼ teaspoon of the salt. Cook, stirring occasionally with a wooden spoon, for 10 to 12 minutes, until very tender. Stir in the garlic and ginger, reduce the heat to medium, and cook for 2 to 3 minutes more, stirring often, until just beginning to caramelize.

Add the cumin and garam masala and cook, stirring, for 30 seconds. Add the tomatoes, 1 cup of the water, the cayenne pepper, black pepper, and ¾ teaspoon of the salt. Let the mixture come to a boil, then reduce the heat so it simmers, cover tightly, and cook for 15 minutes.

Meanwhile, bring a medium saucepan full of water to a boil over medium-high heat. Add the lentils. Reduce the heat so it simmers and cook for about 25 minutes, or until tender. Drain into a strainer.

To make the rice, bring the remaining 1½ cups water and ⅛ teaspoon salt to a boil. Stir in the rice. Cover tightly and reduce the heat to low. Cook for 15 minutes. Remove from the heat, fluff with a fork, and let stand, covered, for 5 minutes more.

Using a handheld blender or regular blender, puree the tomato mixture until creamy and smooth. If it's a little thick, add a little more water. Stir in the lentils. Taste for salt; you may want to add a little more.

Serve the lentils with rice and top with dill and a squeeze of lime.

Mushroom Toast

This is a stand-out. We adapted this after trying
a very buttery, creamy version at a favorite spot in Durham,
North Carolina. This one is just as good.

Active: 30 min / Total: 30 min / Serves 4

2 pounds mixed mushrooms, such as button, shiitake, and oyster

¼ cup extra virgin olive oil, plus more for the baguette

2 large shallots, chopped

¾ teaspoon kosher salt, plus more to taste

2 cloves garlic, finely chopped

2 teaspoons fresh thyme leaves

⅓ cup brandy or dry white wine, such as pinot grigio

¼ teaspoon freshly ground black pepper

1 baguette

12 fresh chives

Wipe the mushrooms with a damp paper towel to remove any dirt. For the button mushrooms, cut them into quarters. For the shiitake mushrooms, pull off the stems and discard, then thinly slice the caps. For the oyster mushrooms, cut away the tough stems and discard, then cut the caps into 1-inch pieces. This will look like way too many mushrooms, but they will cook down.

In a large wide-bottomed pot or Dutch oven, heat the oil over medium-high heat. Add the shallots and ¼ teaspoon of the salt and cook, stirring often, for about 3 minutes, or until tender. Add the garlic and cook, stirring, for 30 seconds, or until fragrant.

Add the mushrooms and stir to coat. Now let them cook, without stirring, for 2 to 3 minutes, until they begin to brown. Then, stir occasionally as they cook for about 5 minutes more. They will first release their liquid; continue to cook the mushrooms until the liquid cooks away. Add the thyme and brandy and cook, stirring often, until the brandy cooks away. Stir in the remaining ½ teaspoon salt and the pepper. Taste for salt; you may want to add a little more.

Position a rack about 6 inches from the top of the oven. Heat the broiler to high.

Cut the baguette in half crosswise, then cut it in half lengthwise. Brush the cut sides with some oil and place, cut sides up, on a sheet pan. Broil for 2 to 3 minutes, until golden brown and toasted.

Cut the toasted baguette into smaller pieces and spoon on the mushrooms. Use scissors to snip the chives over the tops.

Grilled Broccoli with Quinoa Salad and Lemon Tahini Dressing

Remember how we talked about reimagining your plate?
This is an entire, perfect meal, right here. Don't miss out.

Active: 35 min / Total: 35 min / Serves 4

For the quinoa salad

2½ cups water

1¼ cups quinoa

1 pint cherry or grape tomatoes, quartered, or 2 beefsteak tomatoes, diced

4 scallions (white and light green parts), thinly sliced

3 tablespoons chopped fresh flat-leaf parsley

2 tablespoons chopped fresh mint

3 tablespoons extra virgin olive oil

½ teaspoon kosher salt, plus more to taste

¼ teaspoon freshly ground black pepper

For the broccoli

2 bunches of broccoli

4 tablespoons extra virgin olive oil

¼ teaspoon kosher salt

¼ teaspoon freshly ground black pepper

¼ teaspoon crushed red pepper flakes

1 recipe Lemon Tahini Dressing (page 211)

Make the quinoa salad: In a medium saucepan, bring the water to a boil over medium-high heat. Stir in the quinoa. Once it comes back to a boil, cover tightly, reduce the heat to low, and cook for 12 to 15 minutes, until the water is absorbed and the quinoa is tender. Remove from the heat. Fluff with a fork, then let stand, covered, for 5 minutes more. Remove the lid and let cool.

In a large bowl, combine the quinoa, tomatoes, scallions, parsley, mint, oil, salt, and pepper and stir together. Taste for salt; you may want to add a little more.

Heat the grill to medium-high.

Make the broccoli: Trim the stems of the broccoli but leave about 3 inches of the stem attached to the crown. Cut the broccoli lengthwise from top to bottom into ¼-inch-thick slices. It's okay if a few small florets detach. Place the slices and florets on a rimmed sheet pan and drizzle with the oil. Sprinkle with salt, black pepper, and red pepper flakes and toss to coat.

Grill the broccoli for 3 to 5 minutes per side, until charred and tender. Alternatively, you could broil the broccoli.

Serve the broccoli over the quinoa salad and drizzle with the Lemon Tahini Dressing.

Eggplant Cutlets

A cutlet is universally popular. We make it vegan
by replacing eggs with aquafaba (the liquid from a can
of chickpeas—or, as I call it, "goo").

Active: 30 min / Total: 30 min / Serves 4

One 15.5-ounce can chickpeas

½ cup all-purpose flour, spooned and leveled

1½ cups panko or dried plain breadcrumbs

3 tablespoons chopped fresh flat-leaf parsley

1¼ teaspoons kosher salt, plus more for the salad

¼ teaspoon freshly ground black pepper, plus more for the salad

1 large eggplant (about 1½ pounds)

Extra virgin olive oil, for frying, plus more for the salad

4 cups arugula, for the salad

1 cup halved cherry tomatoes, for the salad

½ small red onion, very thinly sliced, for the salad

Lemon wedges, for serving

Drain the chickpeas into a strainer placed over a bowl and reserve the aquafaba (you should get about ¾ cup). Rinse the chickpeas.

Set up your breading station: Arrange three shallow bowls in a row on your counter. To the first bowl, add the flour, and to the middle bowl, add the aquafaba. In the last bowl, combine the breadcrumbs, parsley, salt, and pepper. Place a large plate to the side.

Trim the top and bottom of the eggplant. Slice the eggplant into rounds a little less than ½ inch thick.

Using one hand, dredge each eggplant slice in the flour, then in the aquafaba. Let any excess aquafaba drip off before dipping into the breadcrumb mixture, pressing to help the breadcrumbs adhere. Place on the plate.

In a large skillet, heat ¼ inch of oil over medium-high heat. Test the oil: drop in a few breadcrumbs, and if it sizzles, it's hot. Add a single layer of the cutlets without overcrowding. Cook for 3 to 4 minutes, until the undersides are golden brown and crisp. Flip the cutlets and cook for 2 to 3 minutes more, until golden brown all around. Transfer to a paper towel–lined plate. Repeat with more oil and the remaining eggplant.

Divide the cutlets among plates and alongside arrange a salad of arugula, tomatoes, onion, and a few chickpeas. Drizzle the salad with some oil and sprinkle with a little salt and pepper. Serve with lemon wedges.

Cold Peanut Noodles

These are what you want for a desk lunch,
a picnic in the park, or eating in front of the television.
They are perfect and so are you.

Active: 15 min / Total: 25 min / Serves 4

1 pound spaghetti or soba noodles

¼ cup lower-sodium tamari or
lower-sodium soy sauce

¼ cup smooth peanut butter

2 tablespoons unseasoned rice
vinegar

2 tablespoons toasted sesame oil

1 tablespoon Sriracha, plus more for
serving

1 tablespoon dark brown sugar

1 tablespoon grated peeled fresh
ginger

Small pinch of kosher salt

1 cucumber

3 scallions (white and light green
parts), thinly sliced

⅓ cup chopped roasted, salted
peanuts

Cook the noodles according to the package directions. Drain into a colander and pass under cold running water to cool. Shake out excess water.

In a large bowl, whisk together the tamari, peanut butter, vinegar, sesame oil, Sriracha, brown sugar, ginger, and salt. Add the noodles and toss well to coat.

Quarter the cucumber lengthwise, then slice it crosswise into small pieces.

Divide the noodles among bowls. Top with the cucumber, scallions, peanuts, and a little more Sriracha, if you like extra heat.

Tomato, Mushroom, and Pepperoncini Pizza

This pizza is so delicious, you will not remember
there used to be cheese on your pie. Some of you know,
I like to pop by my local pizza parlor to buy their fresh
dough when I don't have time to make my own.

Active: 25 min / Total: 45 min / Serves 4

For the pizza

1 pound pizza dough (store-bought or homemade), at room temperature

All-purpose flour, for dusting

1 cup cherry tomatoes, halved or quartered, if large

8 ounces medium button mushrooms, very thinly sliced

1 small red onion, very thinly sliced into rings

¼ cup sliced jarred pepperoncini peppers

2 tablespoons extra virgin olive oil, plus more for the pan

½ teaspoon dried oregano

¼ teaspoon kosher salt

⅛ teaspoon freshly ground black pepper

Fresh basil leaves, for serving

For the sauce

One 28-ounce can whole peeled tomatoes

1 clove garlic, grated

2 tablespoons extra virgin olive oil

1 teaspoon dried oregano

¼ teaspoon kosher salt

Heat the oven to 500°F.

Make the pizza: Cut the pizza dough in half and shape into 2 balls. Lightly dust with flour, cover them with a cloth, and let rest.

While the dough rests, make the sauce: Lift the tomatoes out of their juice and put the tomatoes, garlic, oil, oregano, and salt in a blender (save the remaining tomato juice from the can for another use). Blend. This makes more than enough sauce; you can freeze the extra for the next time you make pizza.

In a medium bowl, stir together the cherry tomatoes, mushrooms, onion, pepperoncini, oil, oregano, salt, and pepper.

Once the dough is pliable, use your hands (or a rolling pin) to flatten and stretch it into 10-inch roundish disks. Place them on a lightly oiled sheet pan.

Using the back of a spoon, spread about 3 tablespoons of sauce over each round of dough, leaving a ½-inch border. Dividing evenly, scatter the mushroom mixture over the pizzas.

Bake for 15 to 20 minutes, until the crust is golden brown and crisp underneath. Transfer to a cutting board and slice. Top with basil leaves.

Tomato,
Mushroom, and
Pepperoncini
Pizza, page 119 ▸

Mushroom Bolognese

A meatless makeover for a Seinfeld family favorite.
Use a food processor to chop the vegetables to cut down
on the work. (If you prefer not to use a food processor,
chop the vegetables into pieces of a similar size so they
will cook evenly.) Serve this sauce over anything:
pasta, polenta, toasted bread.

Active: 45 min / Total: 45 min / Serves 4 to 6

1 medium yellow onion, cut into quarters

3 tablespoons extra virgin olive oil, plus more for serving

1¼ teaspoons kosher salt, plus more to taste

3 ribs celery, cut into 1-inch pieces

2 medium carrots, cut into 1-inch pieces

4 cloves garlic

1½ pounds button mushrooms

2 tablespoons tomato paste

½ cup dry white wine, such as pinot grigio

One 28-ounce can whole peeled tomatoes

¼ teaspoon freshly ground black pepper

¼ teaspoon crushed red pepper flakes

¼ teaspoon grated nutmeg

3 tablespoons chopped fresh flat-leaf parsley

Put the onion in a food processor and chop. In a large pot or Dutch oven, heat the oil over medium-high heat. Add the onion and ¼ teaspoon of the salt. Cook, stirring occasionally, for 5 to 6 minutes, until softened.

While the onion cooks, chop the celery and carrot in the food processor. Add to the pot and cook, stirring often, for 5 to 7 minutes, until tender. Then finely chop the garlic in the food processor and add to the pot. Cook, stirring, for 1 to 2 minutes, until fragrant.

In two batches, coarsely chop the mushrooms in the food processor into about ¼-inch pieces.

Add the mushrooms to the pot. Cook, stirring occasionally, for 6 to 8 minutes, until all of the liquid releases from the mushrooms, then cooks away completely. Stir in ¼ teaspoon of the salt. Add the tomato paste and cook, stirring, for 1 minute. Stir in the wine and let it simmer away for 1 minute.

Add the tomatoes, black pepper, red pepper flakes, nutmeg, and the remaining ¾ teaspoon salt. Break up the tomatoes with a spoon. Reduce the heat so the sauce simmers, then cover partially with a lid. Cook, stirring occasionally, for 15 to 20 minutes, until the flavors have developed. Stir in the parsley. Taste and adjust the seasoning to your liking; you might want to add a little more salt or red pepper flakes.

Crunchy Vegetable and Peanut Pot Stickers

These taste better than takeout. Grab a child or mate
to make this a fun afternoon project.

Active: 40 min / Total: 40 min / Serves 4

For the sauce

¼ cup lower-sodium tamari or
lower-sodium soy sauce

2 tablespoons toasted sesame oil

2 to 3 teaspoons Sriracha

¼ cup plus 2 tablespoons water

1 tablespoon grated peeled fresh
ginger

For the pot stickers

1 red bell pepper, cored, seeded, and
cut into ¼-inch dice

½ cup frozen shelled edamame,
thawed and chopped

1 cup frozen corn, thawed

1 teaspoon Sriracha

24 square or round wonton
wrappers

Extra virgin olive oil, for cooking

¼ cup chopped roasted peanuts, for
serving

3 tablespoons chopped fresh
cilantro, for serving

3 scallions (white and light green
parts), thinly sliced, for serving

Make the sauce: In a small bowl, stir together the tamari, sesame oil, 2 teaspoons of the Sriracha, the 2 tablespoons water, and the ginger. Add a little more Sriracha, if you like it spicier.

Make the pot stickers: In a medium bowl, stir together the bell pepper, edamame, corn, and Sriracha.

Spread half of the wonton wrappers out on a clean work surface. Place a tablespoon of the filling onto the center of each wrapper. Moisten the edges with water, fold over, and pinch the edges tightly together to seal. Repeat with the remaining filling and wrappers.

Before you start cooking the pot stickers, be sure to prep the peanuts, cilantro, and scallions.

Cooking in batches, in a large nonstick skillet, heat 1 tablespoon of oil over medium-high heat. Add a single layer of pot stickers (it's okay if they touch). Cook for about 1 minute, until the undersides are golden brown. Use tongs to flip them. Then add the ¼ cup water and quickly cover with a tight-fitting lid. Steam for 3 to 4 minutes, until the pot stickers are tender. Divide among bowls. Wipe out the skillet and repeat the process with the remaining pot stickers. (Or if you can manage cooking with two skillets at the same time, do it. It'll speed things up.)

Divide the pot stickers among plates. Drizzle the sauce over the pot stickers and top with the peanuts, cilantro, and scallions.

Glazed Ginger-Barbecue Tofu

If you do tofu, this is your new favorite. Serve over a bowl
of rice, or sautéed spinach, or cooked green beans.

Active: 20 min / Total: 20 min / Serves 4

One 14-ounce package extra-firm or firm tofu, drained

¼ cup lower-sodium tamari or lower-sodium soy sauce

3 tablespoons of your favorite vegan barbecue sauce

3 tablespoons water

1 tablespoon unseasoned rice vinegar

2 teaspoons toasted sesame oil

2 tablespoons grated peeled fresh ginger

¼ teaspoon crushed red pepper flakes (optional)

Extra virgin olive oil, for frying

⅔ cup cornstarch

2 scallions (white and light green parts), thinly sliced

1 tablespoon toasted sesame seeds

Cut the tofu into 1-inch cubes. Place between several layers of paper towels and weigh down with a sheet pan and a can of tomatoes (or a different heavy can) to absorb excess liquid.

In a small bowl, combine the tamari, barbecue sauce, water, vinegar, sesame oil, ginger, and red pepper flakes, if using.

In a large nonstick skillet, heat ¼ inch of olive oil over medium-high heat.

Put the cornstarch in a medium bowl. Add the tofu pieces and toss to coat. Shake off the excess cornstarch and add the tofu, one by one, to the oil. Cook for 3 to 4 minutes on one side, until a light golden-brown crust forms. Carefully turn them and cook the opposite sides for 3 to 4 minutes more. Transfer to a paper towel–lined plate.

Pour the hot oil into a heat-proof container and let cool before discarding. Wipe the skillet clean with a paper towel. Return it to medium heat and add the sauce to the skillet. Once it starts to simmer, add the tofu and stir to coat. The sauce will quickly thicken into a glaze. Stir a few more times to coat, then slide the tofu onto a serving plate. Top with the scallions and sesame seeds.

Cauliflower Curry

Comfy, cozy, and totally satisfying.

Active: 35 min / **Total: 50 min** / **Serves 4**

4 tablespoons extra virgin olive oil

2 medium yellow onions, thinly sliced

1¼ teaspoons kosher salt

2-inch piece of fresh ginger, peeled and sliced

2 cloves garlic, smashed and peeled

1 jalapeño, halved (and seeded if you don't like heat)

Basmati rice, for serving (optional)

2 tablespoons tomato paste

1 tablespoon curry powder

One 13.5-ounce can coconut milk

¾ cup water

1 large head of cauliflower, cut or broken into small florets

1 cup sugar snap peas, thinly sliced, for serving

Chopped roasted cashews, for serving

Chopped fresh cilantro, for serving

Lime wedges, for serving (optional)

In a large pot or Dutch oven, heat 3 tablespoons of the oil over medium-high heat. Add the onions and ½ teaspoon of the salt and stir to coat. Cover tightly and cook for 5 to 6 minutes, until the onions are softened. Remove the lid. Continue to cook the onions for about 12 minutes, stirring often, or until very tender and just beginning to caramelize.

While the onions cook, put the ginger, garlic, jalapeño, and the remaining 1 tablespoon oil in a food processor and pulse into a paste.

If you're making the rice, start it now.

Add the ginger paste to the onions and cook, stirring and scraping the bottom of the pot with a wooden spoon, for 1 to 2 minutes, until fragrant. Add the tomato paste and curry powder and cook, stirring and scraping, for about 30 seconds.

Stir in the coconut milk, water, and the remaining ¾ teaspoon salt. Add the cauliflower and stir to coat. Let come to a boil. Reduce the heat so the sauce simmers, cover tightly, and cook for 12 to 15 minutes, until the cauliflower is tender.

Divide the curry among bowls and top with the sugar snap peas, cashews, and cilantro. Serve with the rice and lime wedges, if using.

Sweet Potato Tacos with Corn Salsa

These gorgeous tacos take less than 30 minutes to make. While the filling roasts, make your fresh corn salsa.

Active: 25 min / **Total: 25 min** / **Serves 4**

For the tacos

- 1½ pounds sweet potatoes, peeled and cut into just under ½-inch cubes
- 2 poblano peppers, halved lengthwise, cored, seeded, and sliced crosswise into ½-inch-thick strips
- 3 tablespoons extra virgin olive oil
- ¾ teaspoon kosher salt

For the salsa

- 1½ cups fresh corn (from about 2 ears)
- ¼ medium red onion, chopped
- 3 tablespoons chopped fresh cilantro
- 2 tablespoons extra virgin olive oil
- 1 tablespoon fresh lime juice
- ⅛ to ¼ teaspoon chipotle powder
- ¼ teaspoon kosher salt

Eight 5- to 6-inch corn tortillas

1 avocado, sliced

Hot sauce, for serving

2 limes, cut into wedges, for serving

Heat the oven to 425°F.

Make the tacos: Put the sweet potatoes and poblanos on a rimmed sheet pan. Drizzle with the oil and sprinkle with the salt. Toss to coat and spread in a single layer. Roast for 20 to 25 minutes, until tender.

Make the salsa: In a medium bowl, stir together the corn, onion, cilantro, oil, lime juice, chipotle powder, and salt.

To heat the tortillas, turn the flame on your stove to medium-high. Using tongs, grab a tortilla and drag it over the burner grate, flipping it, until lightly charred on both sides but still pliable. (Alternatively, heat the tortillas in a dry medium skillet over medium-high heat.)

Fill the tortillas with the sweet potato mixture, corn salsa, and a slice of avocado. Serve the tacos with hot sauce and a couple wedges of lime.

Baked Beans

I would call this a very worthwhile weekend project because
it takes time to make a pot of luscious classic baked beans.
The good news is that you will impress any meat-eaters when
you bring these to a barbecue or winter dinner party.

Active: 10 min / **Total: 3 hrs 10 min (plus soaking time)** / **Serves 6 to 8**

1 pound dried navy beans

⅓ cup packed dark brown sugar

⅓ cup unsulphured molasses

2 tablespoons extra virgin olive oil

1 tablespoon lower-sodium tamari or lower-sodium soy sauce

2 teaspoons dried mustard

1 teaspoon smoked paprika

1 teaspoon kosher salt

¾ teaspoon freshly ground black pepper

1 bay leaf

1 medium yellow onion, cut into 6 wedges

1 tablespoon apple cider vinegar

Follow the quick soak method for dried beans on page 226.

Heat the oven to 300°F.

In a large oven-safe pot or Dutch oven, combine the soaked (drained and rinsed) beans, brown sugar, molasses, oil, tamari, dried mustard, smoked paprika, salt, pepper, bay leaf, and onion. Add enough water to cover the beans by ½ inch. Stir well.

Place over high heat and let come to a boil. Cover tightly and transfer the pot to the oven. Cook the beans for 2 hours. Remove the lid. The liquid should just barely cover the beans. Add a little more water, if it doesn't.

Continue to cook, uncovered, for 1 hour more, or until the beans are tender and the liquid has reduced to just a little below the surface. Remove the pot from the oven and stir to break up the onion, then stir in the vinegar. Let the beans stand for about 10 minutes (this will give the liquid a chance to thicken). Discard the bay leaf. Stir again before serving.

Broccoli Pesto Pasta

My kids' first vegan meal that they didn't know
was vegan. Even better, your vegetable is built in,
so your weeknight meal is complete.

Active: 25 min / Total: 25 min / Serves 4 to 6

2 cups fresh or frozen small broccoli
florets

¾ teaspoon kosher salt, plus more
for pasta water and to taste

2 cloves garlic, smashed and peeled

⅓ cup pine nuts

¼ teaspoon freshly ground black
pepper, plus more for serving

⅛ teaspoon crushed red pepper
flakes

1½ cups packed fresh basil leaves

½ cup extra virgin olive oil

1 pound pasta, such as bucatini

1 tablespoon nutritional yeast
(optional)

If using fresh broccoli, bring a large pot of water to a boil, then salt it. Add the broccoli and cook for 3 to 4 minutes, until tender. Prepare a medium bowl full of ice water. Use a strainer to scoop out the broccoli and add to the ice water to cool. Remove from the ice water and pat dry. (Alternatively, you can use frozen broccoli. To thaw, put in a strainer and pass under tepid running water; shake out excess water and pat dry.)

Let the pot of water return to a boil for the pasta.

In a food processor, combine the garlic, pine nuts, broccoli, the ¾ teaspoon salt, the black pepper, and the red pepper flakes. Pulse until finely ground, scraping down the sides as necessary. Add the basil. With the processor running, drizzle in the oil (the pesto will be a little thick).

Add the pasta to the boiling water and cook according to the package directions. Right before you drain the pasta, reserve 1 cup of the pasta water.

Return the pasta to the pot. Stir in the pesto and as much of the pasta water as needed to make the mixture nice and creamy. Taste for salt; you may want to add a little more. Stir in the nutritional yeast, if using. Serve topped with black pepper.

Stuffed Sweet Potatoes with Cabbage Slaw and Spicy Peanut Dressing

This is a must! A trifecta of sweet (potato), spicy (peanut dressing), and crunchy (cabbage).

Active: 20 min / **Total: 1 hr 10 min** / **Serves 4**

4 medium sweet potatoes

4 cups shredded purple cabbage

¼ cup chopped fresh cilantro

2 scallions (white and light green parts), thinly sliced

1 recipe Spicy Peanut Dressing (page 219)

Chopped peanuts, for serving

Heat the oven to 400°F.

Pierce the sweet potatoes several times with a fork. Place on a rimmed sheet pan and bake for 40 to 50 minutes, until a paring knife slides easily into the center.

Put the cabbage in a large bowl. Add the cilantro and scallions and toss.

Slice the potatoes down the middle and let cool off for a few minutes so they're not piping hot.

Fill the potatoes with the slaw and top with a few spoonfuls of the Spicy Peanut Dressing and some peanuts.

Black Bean Tostadas with Pickled Cabbage

You will love everything that's happening here: crispy tortilla, creamy beans, and pickled cabbage and onion.

Active: 45 min / Total: 45 min / Serves 4

For the pickled cabbage

6 cups shredded green cabbage

1 small red onion, very thinly sliced into rings

1 jalapeño, very thinly sliced into rings (and seeded if you don't like heat)

1 cup white wine vinegar

3 tablespoons sugar

½ teaspoon kosher salt

1 cup water

For the beans

2 tablespoons extra virgin olive oil

½ medium yellow onion, finely chopped

¼ teaspoon kosher salt

1 teaspoon ground cumin

One 15.5-ounce can black beans, drained and rinsed, or 1¾ cups cooked black beans

¼ teaspoon chipotle powder

1 cup water

For the tostadas

Four 5- to 6-inch corn tortillas

1 tablespoon extra virgin olive oil

1 avocado, sliced, for serving

Fresh cilantro leaves, for serving

Heat the oven to 375°F.

Make the pickled cabbage: Place the cabbage, onion, and jalapeño in a medium bowl.

In a small saucepan, combine the vinegar, sugar, salt, and water over medium-high heat and let it come to a boil. Once the sugar is dissolved, pour over the cabbage mixture. Let cool for 10 minutes, then refrigerate for at least 20 minutes, stirring occasionally. (This can be done a day in advance, if you like.)

Make the beans: In a medium saucepan, heat the oil over medium-high heat. Add the onion and salt and cook, stirring occasionally, for 5 to 6 minutes, until softened. Add the cumin and cook, stirring, for 30 seconds. Add the beans, chipotle powder, and water. Reduce the heat to medium and simmer for 10 minutes. Use a handheld or regular blender or the back of a fork to puree or mash the beans. Keep warm.

Heat the tortillas: Lay the tortillas on a sheet pan and brush both sides with the oil. Bake for 12 to 15 minutes, until crisp.

Build your tostadas: Dividing evenly, spread the beans over the tortillas. Use tongs to lift out some of the pickled cabbage mixture, shaking off excess brine, and lay it over the beans. Top with sliced avocado and cilantro.

Creamy Cannellini Bean Rigatoni

Nobody will believe you that this creamy, garlicky meal is vegan.

Active: 15 min / Total: 25 min / Serves 4 to 6

¾ teaspoon kosher salt, plus more for pasta water and to taste

1 pound pasta, such as rigatoni

¼ cup pine nuts

3 tablespoons extra virgin olive oil, plus more for serving

2 cloves garlic, finely chopped

¼ teaspoon crushed red pepper flakes

One 15.5-ounce can cannellini beans, drained and rinsed, or 1½ cups cooked cannellini beans

¼ teaspoon freshly ground black pepper, plus more for serving

2 tablespoons nutritional yeast (optional)

12 fresh basil leaves, for serving

1 lemon, for serving

Bring a large pot of water to a boil, then salt it. Add the pasta and cook according to the package directions. Right before you drain the pasta, reserve 1 cup of the pasta water.

While the pasta cooks, put the pine nuts in a small dry skillet over medium heat. Cook for 3 to 5 minutes, tossing often, until golden brown. Remove from the heat.

Once you drain the pasta, wipe the pot dry and return it to medium heat. Add the oil, garlic, and red pepper flakes. Cook, stirring, for 30 seconds, or until the garlic is fragrant but not browned. Add the beans, the ¾ teaspoon salt, and the black pepper, and stir to coat with the oil.

Add ½ cup of the reserved pasta water. Using a potato masher or the back of a fork, mash the beans until they are mostly mashed. Add the pasta and stir well to coat with the beans. Sprinkle in the nutritional yeast, if using, and stir again. If the pasta mixture is a little stiff, stir in some or all of the remaining pasta water to loosen. Taste for seasoning; you may want to add a little more salt.

Divide the pasta among bowls and serve topped with the basil leaves, pine nuts, and a little more oil, then grate on some lemon zest and sprinkle with black pepper.

Roasted Cauliflower Wedges with Ranchero Sauce

It makes people angry when you try to convince
them that cauliflower is an entrée and can be close to a
steak-eating experience. That's just silly. It's even better!
Serve with a steak knife for the full steak effect.

Active: 25 min / Total: 1 hr / Serves 4

2 small heads of cauliflower, cut into quarters through the core

6 tablespoons extra virgin olive oil

½ teaspoon kosher salt

¼ teaspoon freshly ground black pepper

Four 8-inch flour tortillas, for serving (optional)

1 recipe Ranchero Sauce (page 208)

Fresh cilantro leaves, for serving

Roasted pepitas, for serving

Heat the oven to 425°F.

Place the cauliflower quarters on a rimmed sheet pan. Dividing evenly, drizzle with the oil and rub to coat. Sprinkle with the salt and pepper. Roast for 35 to 45 minutes, until golden brown on their sides and tender when pierced with a paring knife. (Halfway through cooking, tip each piece onto its other side for even browning.)

To heat the tortillas, if using, turn the flame on your stove to medium-high. Using tongs, grab a tortilla and drag it over the burner grate, flipping it, until lightly charred on both sides but still pliable. (Alternatively, heat the tortillas in a dry medium skillet over medium-high heat.)

Divide the Ranchero Sauce and cauliflower among plates. Top with cilantro and pepitas. Serve with the tortillas, if using.

Broiled Barbecue Eggplant and Coleslaw Stuffed Pitas

Afraid of missing barbecue in your vegan life?
Look no further.

Active: 30 min / Total: 30 min / Serves 4

For the coleslaw

6 cups shredded green cabbage

½ small red onion, very thinly sliced

½ to 1 jalapeño, quartered lengthwise (and seeded if you don't like heat) and cut into small pieces

½ cup fresh corn (from about 1 ear)

¼ cup chopped fresh flat-leaf parsley

2 tablespoons fresh lime juice

1 tablespoon tahini

1 tablespoon extra virgin olive oil

½ teaspoon ground cumin

¼ teaspoon kosher salt, plus more to taste

⅛ teaspoon freshly ground black pepper

For the eggplant

1 medium-large eggplant

5 tablespoons extra virgin olive oil

1 cup of your favorite vegan barbecue sauce

Four 6- to 8-inch pita breads

Make the coleslaw: In a medium bowl, combine the cabbage, onion, jalapeño, corn, and parsley.

In a small bowl, whisk together the lime juice, tahini, oil, cumin, salt, and pepper. Pour over the cabbage mixture and toss to coat. Taste for salt; you may want to add a little more.

Make the eggplant: Position the oven rack about 4 inches from the top and heat the broiler.

Trim the ends of the eggplant, then peel the skin in alternating strips, so the eggplant looks like it has long stripes. Cut the eggplant into ¼-inch-thick rounds. Lay the slices in a single layer on a rimmed sheet pan. Lightly brush both sides with the oil. Broil for 3 to 5 minutes per side, until golden brown and tender. Now brush the tops of the eggplant slices with half of the barbecue sauce. Broil for about 1 minute, until the sauce starts to char. Flip the eggplant and brush with the remaining barbecue sauce. Broil for about 1 minute more.

Warm the pitas in the oven. Trim off the tops of the pitas and open them. Dividing evenly, fill with the coleslaw and eggplant.

Spicy Noodle Bowl

This is a great meal or side dish for you and your lively crew.
I recommend adding tofu. You can also throw in any
vegetable you want. Broccoli or spinach works great!

Active: 20 min / **Total: 35 min** / **Serves 4**

½ cup extra virgin olive oil

3 tablespoons toasted sesame oil

¼ to ½ teaspoon crushed red
pepper flakes

2 tablespoons grated peeled fresh
ginger

6 cloves garlic, thinly sliced

4 large shallots, thinly sliced

¼ teaspoon kosher salt, plus more
for cooking the noodles

2 tablespoons lower-sodium tamari
or lower-sodium soy sauce

12 ounces curly Japanese or Chinese
noodles (often found in a typical
grocery store)

6 heads of baby bok choy

One 14-ounce package firm or extra-
firm tofu, cut into small cubes and
patted dry (optional)

2 tablespoons toasted sesame
seeds

In a large pot, combine the olive oil, sesame oil, red pepper flakes, ginger, garlic, shallots, and the ¼ teaspoon salt over medium-low heat. Let bubble gently for 20 to 25 minutes, until the shallots and garlic are meltingly soft. Remove from the heat and stir in the tamari.

Meanwhile, fill a large pot with water to 2 inches from the top. Place over high heat and let come to a boil. Cook the noodles according to the package directions; drain into a colander and pass under cold running water to stop the cooking. Shake out excess water.

For the bok choy, first hold each head at the white end and slice the green part of the leaves crosswise into 1-inch-thick strips. Then slice the white part of the leaves into ¼-inch-thick strips.

Place the ginger-garlic mixture over medium heat. Add the bok choy and cook for 3 to 4 minutes, until tender. Stir in the tofu, if using.

Add the noodles and toss together until they are well coated. Sprinkle with sesame seeds and serve hot.

Smoky Bean Chili

It may look like a busy recipe, but you're just adding
a bunch of delicious things to a pot. Make this
year-round and spoon on our Chipotle Cashew Queso,
or top with sliced avocado instead.

Active: 20 min / Total: 45 min / Serves 4

3 tablespoons extra virgin olive oil

1 large yellow onion, chopped

1¼ teaspoons kosher salt, plus more
   to taste

2 cloves garlic, finely chopped

1 tablespoon tomato paste

2 bell peppers (any color), cored,
   seeded, and cut into ½-inch dice

One 14.5-ounce can diced tomatoes

2 teaspoons apple cider or red wine
   vinegar

2 teaspoons chili powder

1 teaspoon smoked paprika

¼ teaspoon chipotle powder

¼ teaspoon freshly ground black
   pepper

1½ cups water

One 15.5-ounce can black beans,
   drained and rinsed, or 1½ cups
   cooked black beans

One 15.5-ounce can kidney beans,
   drained and rinsed, or 1¾ cups
   cooked kidney beans

1 cup fresh or frozen corn (from 1 to
   2 ears, if using fresh)

1 recipe Chipotle Cashew Queso
   (page 208), for serving

Fresh cilantro leaves, for serving

In a large pot or Dutch oven, heat the oil over medium-high heat. Stir in the onion and ¼ teaspoon of the salt. Cook, stirring occasionally with a wooden spoon, for 7 to 8 minutes, until tender. Add the garlic and cook, stirring, for about 1 minute, or until fragrant. Add the tomato paste and cook, stirring, for about 2 minutes to caramelize the tomato paste. Stir in the bell peppers.

Add the tomatoes, vinegar, chili powder, paprika, chipotle powder, black pepper, the remaining 1 teaspoon salt, and the water. Let come to a boil, then reduce the heat and let simmer for 12 to 15 minutes, until the bell peppers are tender. Add the black beans, kidney beans, and corn and simmer, partially covered, for 10 minutes. Taste for salt; you may want to add a little more.

Serve the chili topped with some Chipotle Cashew Queso and cilantro.

Potato Taquitos with Guacamole

This fried and festive meal turns any night at
home into a raging party.

Active: 30 min / Total: 30 min / Makes 12

1¼ pounds medium Yukon Gold or
red potatoes

2 tablespoons extra virgin olive oil,
plus more for frying

½ teaspoon chipotle powder

½ teaspoon kosher salt, plus more
for potato water

Twelve 5- to 6-inch corn tortillas

1 recipe Guacamole (page 218) or
store-bought

1 recipe Pico de Gallo (page 221) or
store-bought salsa, for serving

Put the potatoes in a medium saucepan, cover with cold water by
1 inch, add a good pinch of salt, and place over medium-high heat. Let
come to a boil, then reduce the heat so the potatoes simmer gently.
Cook for 15 to 20 minutes, until a paring knife slides easily into a
potato. Drain and pass under cold running water to cool the potatoes.

Use a paring knife to scrape the skins from the potatoes. Then cut
the potatoes into ¼-inch dice and put in a medium bowl. Add the oil,
chipotle powder, and ½ teaspoon salt. Stir together, mashing a little so
the mixture holds together.

To make the tortillas pliable for rolling, in a dry medium skillet
over medium-high heat, heat them one at a time for about 15 seconds
per side.

Spoon about 2 tablespoons of the potato mixture down the middle of
the tortillas. Roll tightly like a cigar with the seam side down.

In the medium skillet, heat about ¼ inch of oil over medium-high
heat. Add half of the taquitos, seam side down, to the skillet. Cook
for 5 to 6 minutes, turning occasionally, until golden brown and
crispy. Transfer to a paper towel–lined plate to drain. Repeat with the
remaining taquitos.

Serve the taquitos with the Guacamole and Pico de Gallo.

CHAPTER THREE

Quick Fixes

Sometimes you don't want to prepare a
full meal, but you are hungry, or bored and peckish.
Or maybe you are new to cooking vegan food?
These quickies are a nice entry point.

Green Hummus

You may balk—but trust instead.

Active: 10 min / Total: 10 min / Makes about 1¼ cups

One 15.5-ounce can chickpeas, drained and rinsed, or 1½ cups cooked chickpeas

1 cup packed fresh flat-leaf parsley or cilantro leaves

2 scallions (white and light green parts), cut into 1-inch pieces

1 clove garlic

¼ cup extra virgin olive oil

2 tablespoons fresh lemon juice

½ teaspoon kosher salt, plus more to taste

⅛ to ¼ teaspoon cayenne pepper

⅛ teaspoon freshly ground black pepper

Fresh fruit and raw crunchy vegetables, for serving, such as clementines, apples, red bell peppers, cucumbers, carrots, and radishes

In a food processor, combine the chickpeas, parsley, scallions, garlic, oil, lemon juice, salt, cayenne pepper, and black pepper. Puree until creamy. If it's too thick, add a splash of water. Taste for salt; you may want to add a little more. Serve with fruit and raw vegetables.

Plantain Chips

Eat with guacamole or salsa or sprinkle with cinnamon and sugar. Or just eat plain.

Active: 15 min / Total: 15 min / Serves 2

1 green plantain

Coconut oil, for frying

Kosher salt, for serving

Trim the ends of the plantain. Using a paring knife, score the skin lengthwise without cutting into the flesh. Repeat twice more, spacing out evenly. With your fingertips, pry away the skin in sections.

Using a chef's knife or a mandoline, slice the plantain on the diagonal no more than 1/16 inch thick.

In a large nonstick skillet, heat a thin layer of oil over medium-high heat. Lay the plantains in a single layer without overlapping. Cook for 3 to 4 minutes per side, until light golden brown. Transfer to a paper towel–lined plate and immediately sprinkle with a little salt. Repeat with the remaining plantain slices and more oil, if necessary. These are best served warm, but room temperature is okay, too.

Mocha Avocado Mousse

I first debuted avocado chocolate mousse in 2007 in *Deceptively Delicious*. This updated version is less sugary and has a kick of espresso.

Active: 5 min / Total: 5 min / Serves 1 or 2

¼ cup dark chocolate chips (vegan)

2 tablespoons brewed espresso or coffee

1 avocado

2 teaspoons agave nectar

1 teaspoon pure vanilla extract

Small pinch of kosher salt

In a small bowl, combine the chocolate chips and espresso. Heat in a microwave or over a double boiler until the chocolate chips melt; whisk until creamy.

In a food processor or blender, combine the avocado, chocolate mixture, agave nectar, vanilla, and salt. Puree until creamy and luscious.

Rice Crackers with Cream Cheese, Cucumber, and Salsa

Spicy, creamy, and crunchy, this snack looks fancy but is serveable in about 30 seconds.

Active: 5 min / Total: 5 min / Serves 1

2 rice cakes

Plant-based cream cheese (We like Violife and Kite Hill) or chilled Ranch Dressing (page 214)

Several slices of cucumber

Salsa, such as Pico de Gallo (page 221) or store-bought

Spread the rice cakes with a layer of cream cheese. Top with cucumber slices and a spoonful of salsa.

Cinnamon Roasted Pineapple

Inspired by a recipe from my friends at Hu Kitchen, this combo of flavors, served warm, will convince you they were born to be together.

Active: 5 min / **Total: 50 min** / **Serves 4**

1 pineapple

1 teaspoon ground cinnamon

¼ teaspoon flaky sea salt

1 lime, cut into wedges

Heat the oven to 450°F.

Cut off the top and bottom of the pineapple, then trim off the skin. Cut the pineapple into quarters lengthwise and cut the long core from each piece. Then slice the pineapple crosswise into ½-inch-thick pieces.

Put the pineapple pieces on a rimmed sheet pan in a single layer. Sprinkle with the cinnamon. Roast, stirring halfway through, until tender and caramelized, 35 to 45 minutes. Sprinkle with the salt and serve with lime wedges.

Club Sandwich

Everyone loves a club sandwich. Refrigerate the Ranch Dressing so it's thick and spreadable.

Active: 10 min / **Total: 10 min** / **Serves 1**

2 slices whole-grain bread

¼ cup chilled Ranch Dressing (page 214)

3 leaves butter lettuce

½ beefsteak tomato, sliced

¼ cucumber, sliced

¼ avocado, sliced

Pinch of kosher salt

Pinch of freshly ground black pepper

Toast the bread, then spread each slice with the Ranch Dressing. Build your sandwich with the lettuce, tomato, cucumber, avocado, and a little salt and pepper.

How Not to Be an Annoying Vegan

I've learned to assume nothing about how someone relates to food, emotionally and psychologically. Big proclamations and bold mandates do not go far, in my experience.

I don't "should" people. In general, nobody wants to be told what they should and shouldn't do. It's judgy and annoying. I think veganism got a bad rap that way: vegans told people how they must eat, and made you feel like a bad person if you weren't following their rules.

Food is a personal thing. Humans connect food with home, family, memories, traditions, and holidays. Food habits are deeply embedded and connected to our emotional state.

When an individual finds the strength to make a dramatic shift in the way they eat, they often feel proud of this huge accomplishment. By the same token, people like to share good information and their successes with others. Some want to recruit others to join in their new lifestyle. That makes

Nobody wants to be told what they should and shouldn't do.

sense. But some forget when coaxing others that food is a trigger and a deeply rooted connection to the past. "You should eat vegan" is a statement that people hear as a command and it turns them off to an idea worth hearing about.

We all want to feel like we make good choices, and sometimes a vegan comes along and tells us in a subtle or not so subtle way that we are making bad choices. They claim that our choices not only harm our bodies and those of our children but also harm the world. Yikes. That stings.

For a person to move toward veganism, a behavior change is required. It is not as simple as going out and buying fruits and vegetables and nondairy items and *poof!* you're a vegan. You have to rewire your current brain; adapt new patterns, likes, and dislikes; and adjust to a new set of rules. That is hard work and difficult to achieve.

This book is for those of you who have been on the receiving end of too many "you shoulds." Dip a toe in. If you want to dive in, the water is warm. Go at your own pace.

Pita with Za'atar and Cucumber Olive Salad

A quick Middle Eastern pick-me-up.

Active: 15 min / Total: 15 min / Serves 2

½ cup cherry or grape tomatoes, quartered

½ cucumber, cut into ½-inch dice

¼ cup pitted kalamata olives, halved

8 fresh mint leaves, torn

5 tablespoons extra virgin olive oil, plus more if necessary

1 tablespoon fresh lemon juice

¼ teaspoon kosher salt

⅛ teaspoon freshly ground black pepper

¼ cup za'atar spice blend

1 pita bread, warmed

In a medium bowl, combine the tomatoes, cucumber, olives, mint, 1 tablespoon of the oil, the lemon juice, salt, and pepper. Stir to combine.

In a small bowl, stir together the za'atar and the remaining 4 tablespoons oil. It should be spreadable. If it's too thick, stir in a little more oil.

Using a serrated knife, cut around the edge of the pita, then pull it apart.

To assemble, spread the za'atar mixture over the pita rounds and spoon on the salad. Roll up and eat.

Sweet and Spicy Snack Mix

Gluten-free. Addictive. With a little spice.

Active: 10 min / Total: 25 min / Makes about 3 cups

1 cup walnuts, coarsely chopped

½ cup sliced almonds

½ cup chickpea flour, spooned and leveled

¼ cup pure maple syrup

⅓ cup chopped dried apricots

1 tablespoon dark brown sugar

2 teaspoons coconut oil, melted

½ teaspoon smoked paprika

⅛ to ¼ teaspoon cayenne pepper

½ teaspoon kosher salt

Heat the oven to 350°F. Line a rimmed sheet pan with parchment paper.

In a medium bowl, combine the walnuts, almonds, chickpea flour, maple syrup, apricots, brown sugar, oil, paprika, cayenne pepper, and salt. Stir together until well combined.

Press the mixture into an even layer on the prepared pan. Bake for about 12 minutes, or until beginning to brown around the edges. Using a spatula or spoon, break the mixture up into smaller pieces. Bake for 3 to 4 minutes, until crisp. It will crisp up more as it cools.

Cashew-Coconut Bites

These make a great on-the-go breakfast or satisfying snack.

Active: 10 min / Total: 10 min / Makes 22

---

2 cups raw cashews

1 cup unsweetened shredded coconut

2 tablespoons chia seeds

¼ teaspoon kosher salt

¼ cup pure maple syrup, plus more if necessary

In a food processor, pulse together the cashews, ½ cup of the coconut, the chia seeds, and the salt until finely chopped. Add the maple syrup. Pulse a few times to combine. The mixture should hold together when squeezed. If necessary, add a little more syrup.

Put the remaining ½ cup coconut in a bowl.

Scoop out about 1 tablespoon of the mixture and squeeze into a ball. Roll it in the coconut, pressing to help the coconut adhere. Repeat; you should get about 22 balls total.

Peanut Butter Crispy Rice Treats

Use any nut butter you like. And you can always stir in dried fruit or top with melted chocolate. These also make a great topping crumbled over Blueberry V'ice Cream (page 189) or cashew or coconut yogurt.

Active: 10 min / Total: 40 min / Makes 16

½ cup smooth peanut butter

¼ cup pure maple syrup

1 tablespoon coconut oil

½ teaspoon pure vanilla extract

Pinch of kosher salt

3 cups crispy rice cereal

Line the bottom of an 8 x 8-inch baking pan with parchment paper, leaving an overhang on two sides.

In a medium saucepan, combine the peanut butter, maple syrup, oil, vanilla, and salt over medium-low heat. Whisk together until melted and creamy. Remove from the heat.

Add the rice cereal and stir until the cereal is evenly coated. Scrape the mixture into the prepared pan, and, using the back of a spoon, press in firmly and evenly. Refrigerate for about 45 minutes, or until cold and sliceable.

Grab the parchment edges and lift onto a cutting board. Cut into squares. Keep refrigerated or frozen.

Triscuits with Date Butter and Apples

When friends come over for coffee, let them know you care by making these. The ginger does not disappoint.

Active: 5 min / **Total: 15 min** / **Makes 12**

½ cup pitted Medjool or Deglet Noor dates
Boiling water, for soaking the dates
1 teaspoon grated peeled fresh ginger
12 Triscuits (whole wheat crackers)
1 apple, sliced, for topping
Ground cinnamon, for sprinkling

Put the dates in a small heat-proof bowl and cover with boiling water. Let stand for 10 minutes, or until softened. Drain the dates and discard the liquid. In a food processor, puree the dates and the ginger until creamy (like butter).

Top the Triscuits with some of the date butter, a slice of apple, and a sprinkle of cinnamon.

Tomato Toast

Don't skip the garlic part.

Active: 5 min / **Total: 5 min** / **Serves 1**

1 slice of rustic bread, such as ciabatta
Extra virgin olive oil
1 clove garlic, cut in half
2 slices beefsteak tomato
Pinch of dried oregano
Pinch of flaky sea salt
Pinch of freshly ground black pepper
Pinch of crushed red pepper flakes

Toast the bread, then drizzle it with a little oil. Rub the cut sides of the garlic over the toast. Lay the tomato slices on top. Drizzle with a little more oil and sprinkle with oregano, salt, black pepper, and red pepper flakes.

Mango-Blackberry Smoothie

A sweet way to get your spinach.

Active: 5 min / Total: 5 min / Serves 1

1 cup frozen mango pieces
½ cup fresh or frozen blackberries
½ cup fresh spinach
2 tablespoons fresh lime juice
1 tablespoon unsweetened shredded coconut

In a blender, combine the mango, blackberries, spinach, lime juice, and coconut. Blend until smooth. Add water to get it to the consistency you like.

English Muffin with Sweet Potato, Peanut Butter, and Banana

I am very happy to have this any time of day as my meal. And this is a main reason I always keep a baked sweet potato in the fridge, ready to go.

Active: 5 min / Total: 5 min / Serves 2

2 English muffins
1 small baked sweet potato
Peanut butter, for serving
1 banana, sliced, for serving
Strawberry jam, for serving
Ground cinnamon, for serving

Split the English muffins in half and toast them.

Scoop the flesh out of the sweet potato and spread over each English muffin half. Top with peanut butter, the banana, jam, and a sprinkle of cinnamon.

Corn Tortilla with Avocado and Hot Sauce

Sometimes I am just looking for a way to use my favorite hot sauce. This vehicle works every time.

Active: 5 min / **Total: 5 min** / **Serves 1**

One 5- to 6-inch corn tortilla
¼ avocado, sliced
Small pinch of kosher salt
Hot sauce, for serving

To heat the tortilla, turn the flame on your stove to medium-high. Using tongs, grab the tortilla and drag it over the burner grate, flipping it, until lightly charred on both sides but still pliable. (Alternatively, heat the tortillas in a dry medium skillet over medium-high heat.)

Place the avocado on the tortilla and sprinkle with a little salt. Shake on some hot sauce. Fold and eat.

Everything Chickpeas

It's like an everything bagel without the bagel.

Active: 10 min / **Total: 10 min** / **Makes about 1 cup**

One 15.5-ounce can chickpeas, drained and rinsed, or 1½ cups cooked chickpeas
Extra virgin olive oil
1 tablespoon "Everything" seasoning
Pinch of kosher salt

Pour the chickpeas onto a dry dish towel and pat them dry.

In a medium skillet, heat about ⅛ inch of oil over medium-high heat. Add the chickpeas and cook for 8 to 10 minutes, stirring often, until golden brown and crisp. Pour them into a paper towel–lined bowl. Toss with the Everything seasoning and a little salt. Transfer to a serving bowl. Eat them while they're warm.

CHAPTER FOUR

Dessert

Sunny's Mint Chip Ice Cream

You will find it very hard to believe this is
vegan. Chef Sunny Lee is lending us this extraordinary
recipe to share with you.

Active: 15 min / **Total: 1 hr 15 min** / **Makes 1 quart**

One 13.5-ounce can unsweetened coconut milk

Two 5.4-ounce cans unsweetened coconut cream

⅓ cup light golden agave nectar

2 tablespoons coconut oil

1 teaspoon kosher salt

2 teaspoons organic peppermint extract

Green food coloring

1 cup dark chocolate chips (vegan)

In a medium saucepan, combine the coconut milk, agave nectar, coconut cream, coconut oil, and salt over medium heat and let come to a simmer.

Very carefully pour the mixture into a blender and blend for 15 to 20 seconds until the fat is completely emulsified into the milk (this will make a creamier ice cream).

Pour the coconut mixture into a medium bowl and place over a large bowl of ice water. Whisk the mixture to cool down. Add the peppermint extract and food coloring (about 6 drops). Adding the extract when the liquid is cool will keep the flavor of the ice cream "fresher" tasting.

Once the ice cream base is cold, spin it in an ice cream machine according to the manufacturer's directions.

With a rolling pin, smash the chocolate chips into small shards.

Fold the chocolate shards into the ice cream at the end of the spinning process. It should be at soft-serve consistency when adding the chocolate. This will allow for even chocolate distribution in the ice cream.

Serve immediately or freeze for 1 hour more for a firmer ice cream. If you freeze for a longer time it will become quite hard, so you'll have to let the ice cream sit out at room temperature for about 15 minutes, until it becomes scoopable.

Fruit Crumble

Who doesn't want to take a tumble with crispy, crunchy, sweet, lemony fruit crumble?

Active: 20 min / Total: 1 hr 40 min / Serves 6 to 8

For the crisp topping

1½ cups all-purpose flour, spooned and leveled

½ cup old-fashioned rolled oats

⅓ cup granulated sugar

⅓ cup packed dark brown sugar

¼ teaspoon grated nutmeg

¼ teaspoon kosher salt

½ cup plant-based butter (We like Miyoko's), cut into small pieces

For the fruit filling

7 to 8 cups frozen or fresh fruit, such as a mix of blueberries, blackberries, peaches, or nectarines

½ cup granulated sugar

3 tablespoons all-purpose flour

½ teaspoon grated lemon zest

½ teaspoon ground cinnamon

⅛ teaspoon kosher salt

Make the crisp topping: In a large bowl, combine the flour, oats, granulated sugar, brown sugar, nutmeg, and salt. Add the butter and, using a pastry cutter or your fingertips, cut it into the mixture until crumbly. Refrigerate for 40 minutes or freeze for 20 minutes.

Heat the oven to 375°F.

Make the fruit filling: In a large bowl, toss together the fruit, granulated sugar, flour, lemon zest, cinnamon, and salt. Pour into a 2-quart baking dish that's about 2½ inches deep.

Sprinkle the topping over the fruit filling. Place the baking dish on a rimmed sheet pan to catch any juices that may bubble over while baking. Slide into the oven and bake for 45 to 50 minutes, until the topping is golden brown and the fruit is bubbling. Let cool to room temperature before serving. This is best served the same day you make it.

Carrot Cake

I would make this for my non-vegan friends
without hesitation.

Active: 25 min / **Total: 1 hr (plus cooling time)** / **Serves 8**

For the cake

Nonstick vegetable oil cooking spray

½ cup walnuts

1½ cups all-purpose flour, spooned
and leveled

1 teaspoon ground cinnamon

1 teaspoon baking soda

¾ teaspoon kosher salt

1 cup unsweetened applesauce

½ cup extra virgin olive oil

¾ cup granulated sugar

¼ cup packed dark brown sugar

1 teaspoon pure vanilla extract

1 cup grated carrots

½ cup sweetened flake coconut

For the frosting

¾ cup plant-based cream cheese
(We like Violife and Kite Hill)

1 cup confectioners' sugar

½ teaspoon pure vanilla extract

Heat the oven to 350°F. Spray a 9-inch round cake pan with cooking spray. Line the bottom with parchment paper.

Make the cake: Spread the walnuts onto a small baking pan and bake for about 10 minutes, until crisp and fragrant. When cool enough to handle, chop them.

In a medium bowl, whisk together the flour, cinnamon, baking soda, and salt.

In a large bowl, whisk together the applesauce, oil, granulated sugar, brown sugar, and vanilla. Stir in the carrots, coconut, and walnuts. Add the dry mixture and fold it in until thoroughly combined.

Scrape the batter into the prepared pan and spread it evenly. Bake for 36 to 40 minutes, until a toothpick inserted into the center comes out clean and the cake is springy to the touch.

Let cool on a wire cooling rack for 25 minutes. Run a paring knife around the edge of the cake to loosen from the pan, then turn it out onto the rack. Remove the parchment and let cool completely, top side up, on the rack.

While the cake cools, make the frosting: In a medium bowl or the bowl of a stand mixer, using an electric mixer on medium speed, beat together the cream cheese, confectioners' sugar, and vanilla until creamy.

Frost the top of the cake. Refrigerate until the frosting is set. Slice and serve.

Chocolate Chip Chickpea Cookies

This is the version from *Deceptively Delicious*, made vegan.

Active: 20 min / Total: 35 min / Makes 30 cookies

2 tablespoons flaxseed meal

5 tablespoons water

2 cups all-purpose flour, spooned and leveled

½ cup old-fashioned rolled oats

1 teaspoon baking soda

½ teaspoon kosher salt

1 cup packed dark brown sugar

½ cup coconut oil (in solid form)

2 teaspoons pure vanilla extract

One 15.5-ounce can chickpeas or butter beans, drained and rinsed, or 1½ cups cooked chickpeas or butter beans

12 ounces dark chocolate chips (vegan)

Heat the oven to 350°F. Line two rimmed sheet pans with parchment paper.

In a small bowl, stir together the flaxseed meal and water. Let stand for about 10 minutes, or until thickened.

In a medium bowl, whisk together the flour, oats, baking soda, and salt.

In a large bowl or the bowl of a stand mixer, using an electric mixer on medium speed, beat together the brown sugar and oil. Beat in the flaxseed mixture and vanilla until creamy. Mix in the chickpeas and chocolate chips. Reduce the speed to low and mix in the dry ingredients.

Scoop heaping tablespoons of the dough onto the prepared pans, spacing 2 inches apart. Bake for 12 to 15 minutes, rotating the pans halfway through, until golden brown around the edges and set. Let cool on the pan for 5 minutes before transferring the cookies to a wire cooling rack.

Oatmeal Spice Cake with Broiled Coconut Icing

We put together our favorite things to create
another really incredible thing.

Active: 20 min / Total: 40 min / Serves 8

For the cake

Nonstick vegetable oil cooking spray

1 cup old-fashioned rolled oats

1¼ cups boiling water

½ cup extra virgin olive oil

½ cup granulated sugar

½ cup packed dark brown sugar

1 teaspoon pure vanilla extract

1½ cups all-purpose flour, spooned
    and leveled

1 teaspoon baking powder

½ teaspoon baking soda

1 teaspoon kosher salt

1 teaspoon ground cinnamon

¼ teaspoon grated nutmeg

For the icing

¼ cup coconut oil

¼ cup granulated sugar

¼ cup packed dark brown sugar

¼ cup plant-based milk, such as
    cashew, oat, or almond

¼ teaspoon kosher salt

1 cup sweetened flake coconut

½ cup chopped walnuts or pecans

½ teaspoon pure vanilla extract

Heat the oven to 350°F. Spray an 8 x 8-inch baking pan with cooking spray.

Make the cake: In a large bowl, combine the oats and boiling water. Let stand for about 10 minutes, or until the oats are softened and the water is absorbed. Stir well. Stir in the oil, granulated sugar, brown sugar, and vanilla.

Add the flour, baking powder, baking soda, salt, cinnamon, and nutmeg. Stir gently until just combined.

Scrape the batter into the prepared pan and smooth the top. Bake for 26 to 30 minutes, until a toothpick inserted into the center comes out clean and the cake is springy to the touch. Transfer the cake to a wire cooling rack. Poke with the toothpick about 1 inch deep several times all over the *hot* cake.

While the cake bakes, make the icing: In a small saucepan, melt the coconut oil over medium heat. Whisk in the granulated sugar, brown sugar, milk, and salt and continue to whisk until the sugars are dissolved. Boil for 1 to 2 minutes, until slightly thickened. Remove from the heat and stir in the flaked coconut, walnuts, and vanilla.

Position the oven rack about 8 inches from the top and turn the broiler on to high.

Spread the warm icing evenly over the top of the still-hot cake. Broil for 1 to 3 minutes, until the coconut and walnuts are toasted.

Let the cake cool completely before slicing.

Clementine Granita

Fresh-squeezed orange juice is the key here.
Clementine orange juice is even better.

Active: 10 min / Total: 3 hrs / Serves 4

3 cups freshly squeezed clementine
   or mandarin orange juice,
   including pulp

¼ cup sugar

2 tablespoons fresh lemon juice

In a large liquid measuring cup, combine the orange juice, sugar, and lemon juice and stir until the sugar dissolves. Pour into an 8 x 8-inch metal baking pan and put in the freezer.

After about 1 hour, the mixture will start to form ice crystals. Stir to break them up. Freeze for another 45 minutes—it should be more like a slushie at this point—then stir again. Freeze again, without stirring, for about 2 hours more, or until completely frozen.

Use a fork to scrape the orange ice into fine shavings. Serve in cold glasses.

Chocolate Sheet Cake

This cake is easy and family-friendly, and it passed the "this doesn't taste vegan" kid test in my house.

Active: 25 min / Total: 45 min / Serves 20

For the cake

Nonstick vegetable oil cooking spray

½ cup mashed ripe banana (about 1 large)

½ cup extra virgin olive oil

1½ cups granulated sugar

¼ cup packed dark brown sugar

2 teaspoons pure vanilla extract

1 teaspoon apple cider vinegar

2 cups all-purpose flour, spooned and leveled

¾ cup unsweetened cocoa powder

1½ teaspoons baking soda

1 teaspoon baking powder

1 teaspoon kosher salt

1¾ cups water

For the chocolate icing

3 cups confectioners' sugar

½ cup unsweetened cocoa powder

⅛ teaspoon kosher salt

½ cup coconut milk

2 tablespoons coconut oil

½ teaspoon pure vanilla extract

Blackberries, for serving (optional)

Make the cake: Heat the oven to 350°F. Spray an 18 x 13-inch rimmed sheet pan with cooking spray and line the bottom with parchment paper.

In a large bowl, whisk together the banana, oil, granulated sugar, brown sugar, vanilla, and vinegar until smooth.

In a medium bowl, whisk together the flour, cocoa powder, baking soda, baking powder, and salt.

Add half of the water to the banana mixture and whisk together. Add the flour mixture and whisk until just combined, then whisk in the remaining water. The batter will be thin.

Pour the batter into the prepared pan and spread evenly. Bake for 23 to 25 minutes, until a toothpick comes out clean when inserted into the center. Transfer to a wire cooling rack.

While the cake bakes, make the icing: In a medium bowl, whisk together the confectioners' sugar, cocoa powder, and salt.

In a small saucepan, heat the coconut milk and coconut oil until hot but not boiling. Pour into the cocoa powder mixture. Whisk vigorously until creamy and smooth. Whisk in the vanilla.

Drizzle the icing evenly over the *hot* cake. Working quickly, use an offset metal spatula to spread evenly. Let the cake cool completely before slicing into squares. Serve with blackberries, if using.

Blueberry V'Ice Cream

My cat Ramone's foster mother, Beth, and her husband,
Howard, are always looking for a healthy dessert. They love
my peanut butter v'ice cream in *Food Swings*, so I created
this for them and some other dairy-free friends, too.

Active: 5 min / **Total: 2 hrs 5 min** / **Serves 4**

4 bananas

1½ cups frozen blueberries

½ cup peanut butter

1 tablespoon coconut oil

Small pinch of kosher salt

½ cup dark chocolate chips (vegan)

Slice the bananas into ¼-inch-thick rounds and put them in a zip-top
plastic bag. Spread out the slices into a single layer and seal. Freeze
them for at least 2 hours.

In a food processor, combine the frozen bananas, blueberries, peanut
butter, oil, and salt. Let sit for 2 or 3 minutes. Then pulse until thick
and creamy, scraping down the sides of the food processor as necessary.
Add the chocolate chips and pulse several times to break the chips into
smaller pieces. Serve immediately, or freeze for a scoopable ice cream
experience.

Strawberry Pie with Whipped "Cream"

This may be the recipe that convinces you that
vegans can make a traditional dessert favorite better.
Top with a modern whipped "cream."

Active: 40 min / Total: 4 hrs 40 min / Serves 8

For the crust

Nonstick vegetable oil cooking spray

About 16 graham crackers, or as
needed to make 2 cups of crumbs

3 tablespoons sugar

7 tablespoons coconut oil, melted,
plus more if necessary

For the filling

2½ pounds fresh medium
strawberries, hulled and
quartered (about 8 cups)

½ cup sugar

⅛ teaspoon kosher salt

5 tablespoons cornstarch

¼ cup cold water

1 tablespoon fresh lemon juice

For the whipped "cream"

½ cup cold aquafaba (the liquid from
a can of chickpeas)

3 tablespoons confectioners' sugar

½ teaspoon pure vanilla extract

¼ teaspoon cream of tartar

Heat the oven to 350°F. Spray a 9-inch pie plate with cooking spray.

Make the crust: In a food processor, grind the graham crackers.
(Alternatively, you could use a zip-top plastic bag and a rolling pin to
grind the graham crackers.)

Measure 2 cups of the crumbs and put them in a medium bowl, then stir
in the sugar. Add the oil and stir well. The crumbs should be moist and
hold together when pressed against the side of the bowl. If they don't,
add a little more oil.

Scatter the crumbs evenly over the prepared pie plate. Starting in
the middle, use a glass or measuring cup to firmly press down on the
crumbs across the bottom. Use the side of the glass to press up the sides
of the pie plate. Bake for about 10 minutes, or until set. Let cool.

Make the filling: Put 6½ cups of the strawberries in a medium
saucepan. Stir in the sugar and salt and place over medium heat. Cook,
stirring occasionally, for 6 to 7 minutes, until the strawberries start
to simmer and release their juices. Continue to simmer the mixture,
stirring occasionally, for about 10 minutes, or until the strawberries
start to break down.

Continues

Strawberry Pie with Whipped "Cream"

CONTINUED

In a small bowl, stir together the cornstarch and water until the cornstarch is dissolved. While continuing to stir, pour the cornstarch mixture into the simmering strawberry mixture. Cook over medium heat for 2 to 3 minutes, stirring, until thickened. Remove from the heat, stir in the lemon juice, and let cool. You can speed up the cooling by transferring the mixture to a medium bowl and placing it over a large bowl of ice water. Stir often until cool. (You should get just about 3 cups of filling.)

Stir the remaining strawberries into the filling. Pour the filling into the prepared crust. Refrigerate for at least 4 hours, or until set.

Make the whipped "cream": In a medium bowl or the bowl of a stand mixer, using an electric mixer on medium-high speed, beat together the aquafaba, confectioners' sugar, vanilla, and cream of tartar for 3 or 4 minutes, until soft peaks form.

Slice the pie and serve topped with a dollop of the whipped "cream."

Apple Blackberry Pie

How can pie be vegan and good, you ask?
Try this one. You'll see.

Active: 45 min / Total: 2 hrs 30 min / Serves 8

For the crust

2½ cups all-purpose flour, spooned and leveled, plus more for rolling

2 tablespoons sugar

¼ teaspoon kosher salt

1 cup (8 ounces) plant-based butter (We like Miyoko's), cut into small pieces and frozen for about 10 minutes

7 to 8 tablespoons ice water

1 teaspoon apple cider vinegar

For the filling

2¼ pounds apples (about 4), such as Granny Smith, Golden Delicious, or Cortland (or a mix of all three)

1 tablespoon fresh lemon juice

⅓ cup plus 1 tablespoon sugar, plus more for the top

2 tablespoons all-purpose flour

¼ teaspoon ground cinnamon

¼ teaspoon kosher salt

6 ounces (about 1¼ cups) fresh or frozen blackberries

Make the crust: In a food processor, combine the flour, sugar, and salt and pulse to combine. Add the butter and pulse a few times until the butter pieces are the size of peas. Add 6 tablespoons of the ice water and the vinegar. Pulse a few times until the mixture resembles moist crumbs and holds together when pinched. You'll probably have to add the remaining 1 to 2 tablespoons water. (Alternatively, you can use a pastry cutter or two knives rather than a food processor to make the pastry.)

Tear off a large piece of plastic wrap and lay it on your counter. Pour the crumbly mixture onto the wrap and gather it into a large ball. Divide in half. Shape each half into 1-inch-thick disks. Wrap and refrigerate for 30 minutes.

On a well-floured surface, evenly roll out one of the disks of dough to a circle about ¼ inch thick and 12 inches in diameter, occasionally rotating it to help keep its round shape. Sprinkle with a little more flour, both on top and underneath, to prevent sticking. Lay the dough in a 9-inch pie plate and gently press into the corners, leaving the overhang. Refrigerate.

Position the oven rack to the second-lowest position and heat the oven to 425°F.

Continues

Apple Blackberry Pie

CONTINUED

Make the filling: Peel, core, and cut the apples into ¼-inch-thick slices. Put them in a large bowl and add the lemon juice, the ⅓ cup sugar, the flour, cinnamon, and salt. Toss well.

Fill the pie shell with the apples. Add the blackberries to the bowl and toss with the 1 tablespoon sugar. Spread them over the apples.

Roll out the second pastry to a circle 12 inches in diameter. Lay the pastry over the fruit filling. Trim the edges of both crusts so they hang over the edge of the pie plate by ½ inch. Tuck the edges of the top crust underneath the bottom crust so it sits high on the flat edge of the pie plate. Crimp the edges. Freeze for 10 minutes.

Lightly brush the top of the pie with water. Sprinkle with a little sugar. Use the tip of a paring knife to make slits in the top so steam can escape.

Place the pie on a parchment-lined rimmed sheet pan. Bake for 15 minutes, then reduce the oven temperature to 375°F and bake for another 50 to 60 minutes, until the apples can be easily pierced through the slits. If the crust starts to become too brown, protect the edges with foil.

Let cool on a wire cooling rack for 2 to 3 hours before slicing.

Chocolate Pudding

Silky, smooth chocolate pudding. Not too sweet. Made even better with add-ons like Caramelized Bananas (page 20) or crumbled Peanut Butter Crispy Rice Treats (page 164).

Active: 15 min / Total: 2 hrs 15 min / Serves 4

6 tablespoons sugar

¼ cup unsweetened cocoa powder

3 tablespoons cornstarch

¼ teaspoon kosher salt

2 cups unsweetened plant-based milk, such as cashew, oat, or almond

⅓ cup dark chocolate chips or chopped chocolate (vegan)

½ teaspoon pure vanilla extract

In a small saucepan, whisk together the sugar, cocoa powder, cornstarch, and salt. Whisk in ½ cup of the milk until well incorporated and smooth (be sure to get the corners). Whisk in the remaining 1½ cups milk.

Place the saucepan over medium heat. Using a silicone spatula, stir often for 4 to 5 minutes. Once the pudding just starts to bubble, stir constantly for 2 to 3 minutes, until it has thickened and coats the back of a spoon.

Remove the pudding from the heat. Add the chocolate chips and vanilla and whisk until smooth.

Dividing evenly, scoop the pudding into four 6-ounce cups. Wrap tightly with plastic wrap. Refrigerate for at least 2 hours, or until completely chilled and set.

Oatmeal Raisin Cookies

If you're not a raisin person, use vegan chocolate chips instead.

Active: 20 min / Total: 35 min / Makes 28 cookies

3 tablespoons flaxseed meal

2¼ cups old-fashioned rolled oats

1½ cups all-purpose flour, spooned and leveled

1¼ teaspoons ground cinnamon

¾ teaspoon kosher salt

½ teaspoon baking soda

¾ cup coconut oil (in solid form)

¾ cup granulated sugar

½ cup packed dark brown sugar

1½ teaspoons pure vanilla extract

1 cup raisins

Heat the oven to 350°F. Line two rimmed sheet pans with parchment paper.

In a small bowl, stir together the flaxseed meal and 7½ tablespoons water. Let stand for about 10 minutes, or until thickened.

In a medium bowl, whisk together the oats, flour, cinnamon, salt, and baking soda.

In a large bowl or the bowl of a stand mixer, using an electric mixer on medium-high speed, beat together the oil, granulated sugar, and brown sugar until creamy. Beat in the flaxseed mixture and vanilla until creamy. Reduce the speed to low and mix in the dry ingredients. Mix in the raisins.

Scoop heaping tablespoons of the dough onto the prepared pans, spacing 2 inches apart. Bake for 12 to 15 minutes, rotating the pans halfway through, until set around the edges but a little soft in the middle. Let cool on the pans for 5 minutes before transferring the cookies to a wire cooling rack.

Chocolate-Dipped Oranges

The easiest and best treat in the book.

Active: 10 min / Total: 20 min / Makes about 28

½ cup dark chocolate chips (vegan)

3 clementine oranges

1 tablespoon chopped roasted almonds

Pinch of flaky sea salt

Line a sheet pan with parchment paper.

Put the chocolate chips in a small bowl. Melt in a microwave or over a double boiler and stir until smooth and completely melted.

Peel the oranges and pull apart their segments. Dip half of each segment into the chocolate, then place on the prepared pan. Sprinkle the chocolate-dipped ends with the almonds and salt.

Chill for about 10 minutes in the refrigerator, or until set.

Strawberry Cupcakes

These are for Sascha. My picky girl.
But boy, she loves these.

Active: 20 min / Total: 35 min (plus cooling time) / Makes 12 cupcakes

For the cupcakes

10 ounces fresh strawberries (about 16 medium), hulled

½ cup extra virgin olive oil

¾ cup granulated sugar

1 teaspoon pure vanilla extract

1¾ cups all-purpose flour, spooned and leveled

1½ teaspoons baking powder

½ teaspoon baking soda

½ teaspoon kosher salt

¼ cup unsweetened plant-based milk, such as cashew, almond, or oat

For the frosting

1¼ cups freeze-dried strawberries

6 tablespoons plant-based butter (We like Miyoko's), at room temperature

2 cups confectioners' sugar

2 to 3 tablespoons unsweetened plant-based milk, such as cashew, almond, or oat

½ teaspoon pure vanilla extract

Make the cupcakes: Heat the oven to 350°F. Line a 12-cup muffin tin with paper liners.

In a food processor or blender, puree the strawberries until smooth. You'll need 1 cup of puree.

In a large bowl, whisk together the strawberry puree, oil, granulated sugar, and vanilla. Add the flour, baking powder, baking soda, and salt, and gently stir together. Stir in the milk.

Dividing evenly, spoon the batter into the prepared muffin cups.

Bake for 20 to 23 minutes, until puffed and a toothpick comes out clean when inserted into the center. Let cool for 10 minutes on a wire cooling rack before removing the cupcakes from the pan. Let cool completely before frosting.

Make the frosting: In a food processor, grind the freeze-dried strawberries. (Alternatively, you could use a zip-top plastic bag and a rolling pin to grind the strawberries). Measure ¼ cup and add to a medium bowl or the bowl of a stand mixer. Add the butter, confectioners' sugar, 2 tablespoons of the milk, and the vanilla. Using an electric mixer on low speed, mix together until combined. Increase the speed to medium-high and beat until fluffy. If the frosting is stiff, beat in a little more milk.

Frost the cooled cupcakes.

Peanut Butter Bars

My son Julian was slow to embrace the vegan lifestyle
but was quick to jump on these.

Active: 20 min / Total: 1 hr 20 min / Makes 16 bars

For the crust

Nonstick vegetable cooking spray

About 12 graham crackers, or as needed to make 1⅓ cups of crumbs

3 tablespoons sugar

5 tablespoons coconut oil, melted, plus more if necessary

For the filling

1 cup smooth peanut butter

½ cup sugar

1 teaspoon pure vanilla extract

¼ cup unsweetened coconut cream (in solid form)

¼ cup dark chocolate chips (vegan)

3 tablespoons chopped roasted, salted peanuts

Heat the oven to 350°F. Spray an 8 x 8-inch baking pan with cooking spray and line with parchment paper, leaving an overhang on two opposite sides.

Make the crust: In a food processor, grind the graham crackers. (Alternatively, you could use a zip-top plastic bag and a rolling pin to grind the graham crackers.) Measure 1⅓ cups of the crumbs and put them in a medium bowl, then stir in the sugar. Add the oil and stir well. The crumbs should be moist and hold together when pressed against the side of the bowl. If they don't, add a little more oil.

Pour the crumb mixture into the prepared baking pan. Using a glass or a measuring cup, firmly and evenly press the mixture over the bottom of the pan. Bake for about 10 minutes, or until set. Let cool.

Make the filling: In a medium bowl or the bowl of a stand mixer, using an electric mixer, beat together the peanut butter, sugar, and vanilla on medium-high speed until fluffy. Beat in the coconut cream.

Spread the peanut butter mixture evenly over the graham cracker crust. Melt the chocolate in a small bowl in a microwave or over a double boiler. Drizzle it over the peanut butter topping in a random pattern. Sprinkle with the peanuts. Refrigerate for about 1 hour, or until set.

Grabbing both ends of the parchment, lift out the square onto a cutting board. Cut into small squares for serving. Keep the bars refrigerated or frozen.

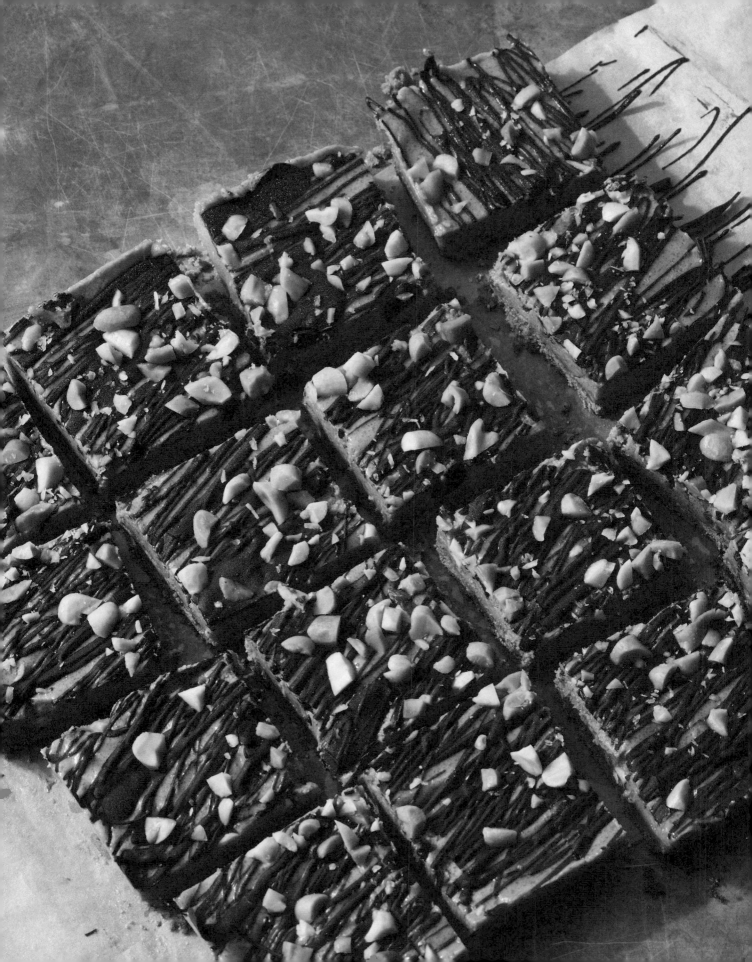

CHAPTER FIVE

Essential Sauces, Dressings, Etc.

Chipotle Cashew Queso

We lean heavily on this recipe, as you can see: you'll find it in Broccoli Quesadillas (page 51), Smoky Bean Chili (page 149), Mexican-Style Grilled Street Corn (page 70), and Roasted, Smashed Potatoes with Fixin's (page 39).

Active: 5 min / Total: 25 min / Makes about 1 cup

1 cup raw cashews

1 canned chipotle pepper in adobo, plus adobo sauce to taste

½ teaspoon kosher salt, plus more to taste

½ cup water, plus more if necessary

Put the cashews in a small saucepan and cover with cold water by 1 inch. Turn the heat on to medium-high. Let come to a boil, then reduce the heat and simmer for 10 minutes. Drain into a colander and pass under cold running water to cool.

Put the cashews in a blender. Add the chipotle, salt, and water. Blend on high speed for about 2 minutes, or until creamy and smooth. If it's too thick, add a little more water for the consistency you like. Taste for salt; you may want to add a little more. You can add a little adobo sauce, too, if you want more smoky heat.

Store in an airtight container in the refrigerator for up to 4 days.

Ranchero Sauce

Great for enchiladas, dipping tortilla chips, and pouring over anything. Try it with Roasted Cauliflower Wedges (page 142) and Roasted Chiles Rellenos (page 59).

Active: 10 min / Total: 25 min / Makes 2¼ cups

½ medium white onion, sliced

1 clove garlic, smashed and peeled

1 tablespoon extra virgin olive oil

½ teaspoon kosher salt, plus more to taste

1½ pounds ripe medium beefsteak tomatoes, cored and halved

1 canned chipotle pepper in adobo, plus adobo sauce to taste

Position the oven rack about 4 inches from the top and heat the broiler.

Place the onion and garlic on a rimmed sheet pan, drizzle with the oil, and sprinkle with ¼ teaspoon of the salt. Toss together and spread into a single layer. Place the tomato halves, cut side down, on the pan as well. Broil for 12 to 15 minutes, occasionally moving everything around, until evenly charred. The more charred the onion is, the better.

Use tongs to peel off the tomato skins and discard. Put the tomatoes and their juices, the onion-garlic mixture, the chipotle, and the remaining ¼ teaspoon salt into a blender and puree until smooth. Taste for salt and spice; you may want to add a little more salt and some of the adobo sauce.

Store in an airtight container in the refrigerator for up to 4 days.

Sriracha Dressing

This is so easy to whip up for Quinoa Patties (page 55) and Kale Quinoa Salad (page 95).

Active: 5 min / **Total: 5 min** / **Makes about 1 cup**

½ cup tahini, well stirred

4 to 6 teaspoons Sriracha

2 tablespoons fresh lime juice

½ teaspoon kosher salt, plus more to taste

6 tablespoons water, plus more if necessary

In a small bowl, whisk together the tahini, Sriracha, lime juice, salt, and water until smooth. If it's too thick, whisk in a little more water. Taste for salt; you may want to add a little more.

Store in an airtight container in the refrigerator for up to 4 days.

Smoky Tahini Dressing

Smoky and creamy, this dressing would be delicious in sandwiches and drizzled over salads but especially with Spice Roasted Sweet Potatoes and Chickpeas (page 87).

Active: 5 min / **Total: 5 min** / **Makes about 1 cup**

½ cup tahini, well stirred

6 tablespoons fresh lemon juice

4 teaspoons smoked paprika

½ teaspoon kosher salt, plus more to taste

¼ cup water, plus more if necessary

In a small bowl, whisk together the tahini, lemon juice, paprika, salt, and water until smooth. If it's too thick, whisk in a little more water. Taste for salt; you may want to add a little more.

Store in an airtight container in the refrigerator for up to 4 days.

Lemon Tahini Dressing

This dressing goes with everything. I love it for Grilled Broccoli with Quinoa Salad (page 112).

Active: 5 min / Total: 5 min / Makes about 1 cup

½ cup tahini, well stirred

6 tablespoons fresh lemon juice

1 clove garlic, grated

½ teaspoon kosher salt, plus more to taste

3 tablespoons water, plus more if necessary

In a small bowl, whisk together the tahini, lemon juice, garlic, and salt. Whisk in the water. If it's still a little thick, whisk in a little more water. Taste for salt; you may want to add a little more.

Store in an airtight container in the refrigerator for up to 4 days.

A Healthy Vegan

You probably know that I am not a doctor. Since I am not in a position to give any kind of medical advice, please consult an actual professional if you decide this vegan lifestyle is for you.

As an armchair doctor, I can tell you that eating dark leafy greens, nuts, seeds, and fortified grains will provide key nutrients, such as protein, iron, vitamin D, calcium, vitamin B12, and omega-3 fats. Our bodies also need vitamin C, zinc, and amino acids. I know you will take responsibility for your own wellness and make sure you are incorporating all of these into your diet.

Many vegans and vegetarians worry about getting enough protein, which is necessary for our bones and muscles and a whole bunch of other important functions that help our bodies grow and repair themselves. Sources of protein include beans, lentils, chickpeas, tofu, dairy-free milks, dairy-free yogurts (cashew and coconut are my favorites), and nuts. You will find lots of ways to eat protein in this book, like our Glazed Ginger-Barbecue Tofu (page 126).

Vitamin B12 helps keep the body's blood cells and nerves healthy. It also supports our DNA function. B12 is not generally found in plants, so some people take it in supplemental form. Though some dairy-free milks are fortified, as well as breakfast cereals. For lunch or dinner make Spaghetti with Olive Oil, Garlic, and Chickpeas (page 102) and be sure to add the nutritional yeast, which is a great source of B12.

Vitamin D keeps our bones and muscles strong and healthy. It also supports our nerves and our immune system. It protects us from osteoporosis, too. On the vegan diet, it is somewhat challenging to derive vitamin D from the foods we eat, but it can be found in mushrooms and in fortified dairy-free milks. Apparently most people are deficient in vitamin D these days, since we spend more time indoors than our ancestors did. To offset, get some more sun.

You probably know that I am not a doctor.

Omega-3 and omega-6 are fats that impact our brains and immune systems. They give your body energy and support your heart, blood vessels, lungs, immune system, and endocrine system. These are important things. You can find these helpful fats in seeds and nuts like flaxseeds, hemp, pepitas (pumpkin seeds), sunflower seeds, walnuts, and tofu. For an omega boost, make the breakfast recipes in this book that use chia seeds.

Calcium, as we have all heard by now, strengthens our bones and teeth. It also helps our muscles and nervous system and clots our blood. Dairy-free milks and yogurts are usually fortified with calcium, as are some tofus; calcium is also found in dark leafy greens like kale, as well as almonds and chia seeds. Lots of recipes in this book will help your calcium uptake.

Iron helps carry oxygen throughout the body. This important mineral is found in fortified breakfast cereals and whole wheat bread, oatmeal, beans, tofu, lentils, spinach, peanut butter, and brown rice. I have read that vitamin C is important in helping to increase the absorption of iron. You can find iron in these recipes: Indian Spiced Lentils and Rice (page 108), Baked Beans (page 133), and Italian White Bean and Farro Soup (page 105).

Ranch Dressing

This is our version of a ranch dressing. Use on Grilled Portobello Burgers (page 82) or serve with Buffalo Cauliflower (page 96). Refrigerate it and it will thicken and become spreadable, perfect for a Club Sandwich (page 158) or a toasted bagel.

Active: 10 min / Total: 10 min / Makes about 2 cups

1 cup blanched whole almonds

1 small clove garlic

½ cup extra virgin olive oil

2 tablespoons fresh lemon juice

1½ teaspoons red wine vinegar

2 teaspoons granulated onion

1 teaspoon kosher salt, plus more to taste

¼ teaspoon freshly ground black pepper

½ cup plus 2 tablespoons water, plus more if necessary

2 tablespoons chopped fresh dill

In a blender, finely chop the almonds and garlic. Add the oil, lemon juice, vinegar, granulated onion, salt, and pepper and blend together. With the blender running, slowly pour in the water and let it run for 2 minutes, until the dressing is nice and creamy. If you want it thinner, add a little more water. Scrape the ranch dressing into a bowl and stir in the dill. Taste for salt; you may want to add a little more.

Store in an airtight container in the refrigerator for up to 4 days.

Ginger-Scallion Relish

So good over Grilled Vegetable Skewers and Coconut Rice (page 74).

Active: 10 min / **Total: 10 min** / **Makes about ¾ cup**

½ cup thinly sliced scallions
(white and light green parts)

2 tablespoons grated peeled fresh ginger

3 tablespoons unseasoned rice vinegar

3 tablespoons extra virgin olive oil

1 teaspoon lower-sodium tamari or
lower-sodium soy sauce

½ teaspoon kosher salt

Small pinch of sugar

In a small bowl, stir together the scallions, ginger, vinegar, oil, tamari, salt, and sugar. Let marinate for at least 10 minutes before using.

Store in an airtight container in the refrigerator for up to 2 days.

House Vinaigrette

Everybody needs a house vinaigrette. This is ours: straightforward with a bite.

Active: 5 min / **Total: 5 min** / **Makes about ¾ cup**

---

1 shallot, finely chopped

¼ cup red wine vinegar

2 teaspoons Dijon mustard

½ cup extra virgin olive oil, plus more if desired

¾ teaspoon kosher salt

¼ teaspoon freshly ground black pepper

1 tablespoon water

In a small bowl or a jar, combine the shallot and vinegar. If you have 10 minutes, let them stand together to take away the bite of the shallot. Then whisk in the mustard, oil, salt, pepper, and water. Taste. If it's a little too sharp for you, add a tablespoon or two of oil to mellow it out. Whisk or shake well before serving.

Store in an airtight container in the refrigerator for up to 7 days.

Roasted Garlic Pesto

The creaminess and sweetness of the roasted garlic make you forget there's no Parmesan. I could eat this by the spoonful. Great for a dip, too. But try it in Roasted Garlic Pesto Pasta Salad (page 88).

Active: 10 min / Total: 50 min / Makes about 1 cup

2 heads of garlic

8 tablespoons plus 2 teaspoons extra virgin olive oil

¼ cup pine nuts

2 cups packed fresh basil leaves

½ teaspoon kosher salt

⅛ teaspoon freshly ground black pepper

Heat the oven to 400°F.

Trim the tops off the garlic heads to expose the cloves, keeping the head intact. Place the garlic heads on a square of foil and drizzle the tops with 1 teaspoon of the oil for each. Seal tightly and roast for 40 to 45 minutes, or until the garlic is very tender.

When cool enough to handle, squeeze out the garlic cloves into a food processor. Add the pine nuts. Pulse a few times to chop.

Add the basil, salt, and pepper. With the food processor running, slowly drizzle in 6 tablespoons of the oil. Scrape down the sides as necessary. The pesto should be nice and creamy. Add the remaining 2 tablespoons oil if it's too thick.

Store in an airtight container in the refrigerator for up to 2 days.

Guacamole

The key to a good guacamole
is a perfect avocado.

Active: 10 min / **Total: 10 min** / **Makes about 2 cups**

2 large avocados

¼ medium white or red onion, finely chopped

½ jalapeño (seeded if you don't like heat),
finely chopped

3 tablespoons chopped fresh cilantro

1 tablespoon fresh lime juice

½ teaspoon kosher salt, plus more to taste

Cut the avocados in half and remove the pits. Score
the flesh in a crosshatch pattern without cutting
through the skin. Scoop out into a medium bowl.

Add the onion, jalapeño, cilantro, lime juice, and
salt. Mash together. Taste for salt; you may want to
add a little more.

Store in an airtight container, with plastic wrap
pressed against the guacamole, in the refrigerator
for up to 1 day.

Peanut Butter Dipping Sauce

Perfect with Vegetable Spring
Rolls (page 77). Delicious made with
cashew butter as well.

Active: 5 min / **Total: 5 min** / **Makes about 1 cup**

½ cup smooth peanut butter or cashew butter

½ cup coconut milk

2 tablespoons fresh lime juice

1 tablespoon Sriracha, plus more to taste

½ teaspoon kosher salt, plus more to taste

In a small bowl, whisk together the peanut butter,
coconut milk, lime juice, Sriracha, and salt. Taste
for salt and spice; you may want to add a little more
salt and Sriracha.

Store in an airtight container in the refrigerator for
up to 4 days.

Spicy Peanut Dressing

A great all-around dressing.
Try with Stuffed Sweet Potatoes with
Cabbage Slaw (page 137).

Active: 5 min / Total: 5 min / Makes about 1 cup

¼ cup lower-sodium tamari or lower-sodium soy
sauce

¼ cup unseasoned rice vinegar

6 tablespoons peanut butter

2 tablespoons toasted sesame oil

2 tablespoons grated peeled fresh ginger

2 to 3 teaspoons Sriracha, plus more to taste

In a small bowl, whisk together the tamari, vinegar,
peanut butter, sesame oil, ginger, and Sriracha.
Taste for heat; you may want to add a little more
Sriracha.

Store in an airtight container in the refrigerator for
up to 4 days.

"Meat"

Crumbly in texture like ground beef
but so much more flavorful and healthy.
Keep on hand for Taco Salad (page 43) and
Loaded Sweet Potato Fries (page 73).

Active: 20 min / Total: 35 min / Makes about 3 cups

¾ cup green or brown lentils, rinsed

2 tablespoons extra virgin olive oil

1 large yellow onion, finely chopped

1 teaspoon kosher salt, plus more to taste

1 tablespoon tomato paste

1 teaspoon smoked paprika

½ teaspoon ground cumin

1½ cups walnuts

¼ teaspoon freshly ground black pepper

Bring a medium saucepan of water to a boil over
medium-high heat. Add the lentils. Reduce the heat
to medium and simmer for about 25 minutes, or until
tender. Drain into a strainer, then pass under cold
running water to cool. Squeeze out excess water.

In a medium skillet, heat the oil over medium-high
heat. Add the onion and ¼ teaspoon of the salt and
cook, stirring often, for 10 to 12 minutes, until very
tender. Add the tomato paste, paprika, and cumin
and cook, stirring, for 1 to 2 minutes to caramelize
the tomato paste. Remove from the heat and let cool.

Put 1½ cups of the cooked lentils, the onion mixture,
walnuts, pepper, and the remaining ¾ teaspoon salt
in a food processor. Pulse several times until crumbly,
not smooth. Taste for salt; you may want to add a
little more.

Store in an airtight container in the refrigerator for
up to 4 days.

Pico de Gallo

When in doubt, put Pico de Gallo on it.
See Black Bean Burgers (page 56), Loaded
Sweet Potato Fries (page 73),
and Taco Salad (page 43).

Active: 10 min / Total: 10 min / Makes about 2 cups

2 medium beefsteak tomatoes (about 1 pound)

¼ medium red or white onion, finely chopped

1 small jalapeño (seeded if you don't like heat),
finely chopped

2 tablespoons chopped fresh cilantro

1 tablespoon extra virgin olive oil

1 tablespoon fresh lime juice

½ teaspoon kosher salt

⅛ teaspoon freshly ground black pepper

Core the tomatoes, then cut them into ¼-inch
dice and place in a medium bowl. Add the onion,
jalapeño, cilantro, oil, lime juice, salt, and black
pepper. Stir together.

Store in an airtight container in the refrigerator for
up to 2 days.

Homemade Croutons

Homemade croutons make everything special.
For instance, Old-School Salad (page 64), Tomato Soup
(page 48), and Stewy White Beans (page 91).

Active: 10 min / Total: 25 min / Makes about 3 cups

12 ounces day-old rustic bread, such as ciabatta or sourdough

1 clove garlic, smashed and peeled (optional)

3 to 4 tablespoons extra virgin olive oil

¼ teaspoon kosher salt

Heat the oven to 400°F.

Cut the crust from the bread. Tear or cut the interior into bite-size pieces (you should get about 4 cups). Put the bread pieces in a medium bowl with the garlic, if using. Drizzle with 3 tablespoons of the oil. With your hands, massage the oil and garlic into the bread pieces. They should be well coated but not soggy. If they seem dry, add the remaining 1 tablespoon oil.

Spread the bread and garlic pieces on a rimmed sheet pan and sprinkle with the salt.

Bake for 10 minutes, then stir the bread around to ensure even baking. Bake for 5 to 8 minutes more, stirring again halfway through, until golden brown and crisp. The garlic bits should be nice and crisp, too.

The croutons will keep in a zip-top plastic bag for up to 2 days. If needed, you can freshen them up in the oven for a few minutes before serving.

Vegetable Broth

Never let a vegetable (or its scraps) go unused.
Here's a basic vegetable broth that's always nice to have on
hand (or in the freezer) for using in soups or risotto.

Active: 5 min / Total: 1 hr 45 min / Makes about 6 cups

4 ribs celery, quartered crosswise

4 medium carrots, quartered
crosswise

1 medium yellow onion, quartered

1 red bell pepper, cored, seeded, and
quartered

1 head of garlic, halved crosswise

Handful of fresh flat-leaf parsley
stems

2 bay leaves

1 tablespoon black peppercorns

2 teaspoons kosher salt

12 cups cold water

In a large pot, combine, the celery, carrots, onion, bell pepper, garlic, parsley, bay leaves, peppercorns, and salt. Add the water. making sure the vegetables are covered. Place over medium-high heat, cover partially with a lid, and let come to a boil. Reduce the heat to medium-low and simmer for 1 hour 15 minutes. Let cool for 15 minutes before straining.

Set a fine strainer over a large container or bowl. Use a ladle to scoop the vegetables into the strainer. Press the vegetables with the ladle to extrude as much broth as possible. Discard the vegetables. Pour the remaining broth through the strainer.

A Dried Beans How-To

Cooking with dried beans is economical and flavorful (I say this with no disrespect to canned beans, which are incredibly convenient). A little time management is required, but it's well worth it once you get the rhythm down. It's nearly impossible to mess up a pot of beans.

Before you do anything, pour the beans into a strainer and sift through them, discarding any debris or beans that look shriveled. Rinse.

Overnight Soak

If you remember to soak your beans overnight, they'll cook faster and more evenly than without a soak. Older beans especially benefit from soaking. No need to soak black beans, pinto beans, or black-eyed peas.

For 1 pound of beans, in a large bowl, dissolve 2 tablespoons kosher salt in 2 quarts cold water. Add the beans, making sure the water covers the beans by 2 inches. Let soak on the counter for at least 4 hours and up to 8 hours. If soaking longer, do so in the refrigerator for at least 8 hours and up to 12 hours. Drain, rinse, then follow the cooking methods.

Quick Soak

If you forget to soak, follow this method:

For 1 pound of beans, in a Dutch oven or large pot, add the beans and cover with cold water by 2 inches. Stir in 2 tablespoons kosher salt. Place over high heat and let come to a boil. Remove the pot from the heat and let stand for 1 hour. Drain, rinse, then follow the cooking methods.

No Soak

It's not the end of the world if you don't soak your beans. You'll just have to cook them 1 to 2 hours longer and monitor the level of water, making sure the beans remain covered by 1 inch. Note that sturdier beans like chickpeas, navy beans, and gigante beans really do benefit from a soak. Black beans, pinto beans, and black-eyed peas do well without a soak as do freshly dried beans.

Stovetop Cooking

Place the beans in the pot and cover with cold water by 3 inches. Season with a pinch of salt. If you have aromatics on hand, like onion, carrot, celery, bay leaf, fresh rosemary, or sage, add them as well (don't add vinegar; it will toughen the beans). This will enhance their flavor, but it's not a make or break. Place the pot over medium-high heat. Once it comes to a boil, reduce the heat to a gentle simmer and cover partially with a lid. Be sure to check the water level as they simmer to make sure the beans remain covered, and stir occasionally. Skim any foam that rises to the surface. Cooking times vary depending on bean variety and age, so the best approach is to taste them from time to time for doneness. You want them to hold their shape but be creamy on the inside, not tough or grainy (make sure to taste a few). Remove from the heat. Let the beans cool to room temperature in their cooking liquid.

Pressure Cooker Cooking

If you want to skip the soak and save time, cook your beans in a pressure cooker. Add the beans to the pot and cover with lightly salted water by 2 inches; add aromatics, if using. Make sure not to fill the pot higher than half full. Follow your pressure cooker guide for cooking times.

Storing Your Beans

If you're not using the cooked beans right away, refrigerate them in their cooking liquid (for up to 5 days). They freeze well this way, too.

Sample Menus

It takes thought, effort, and work to cook a decent meal. Fresh vegetables and fruit are the foundation of vegan food, thus requiring some frequent trips to the grocery store to buy produce. To help you organize, we have devised a little menu plan for you. We created it with busy, working people in mind. Feel free to mix and match.

Seasonal Dinners

SPRING

Roasted, Smashed Potatoes with Fixin's (page 39)

or

Grilled Broccoli with Quinoa Salad and Lemon Tahini Dressing (page 112)

DESSERT: Strawberry Cupcakes (page 203)

SUMMER

Potato Taquitos with Guacamole (page 150)

and

Mexican-Style Grilled Street Corn (page 70)

or

Grilled Portobello Burgers (page 82)

and

Roasted Garlic Pesto Pasta Salad (page 88)

DESSERT: Fruit Crumble (page 177)

FALL

Cauliflower Curry (page 129)

or

Butternut Squash and Quinoa Soup (page 40)

and

Mushroom Toast (page 111)

DESSERT: Apple Blackberry Pie (page 193)

WINTER

Creamy Polenta with Roasted Mushrooms and Tomatoes (page 99)

or

Stewy White Beans (page 91)

DESSERT: Carrot Cake (page 178)

Weekly Meals

MONDAY

BREAKFAST: Overnight Oats (page 30)

LUNCH: Broccoli Quesadillas with Chipotle Cashew Queso (page 51)

SNACK: Cinnamon Roasted Pineapple (page 158)

DINNER: Sloppy Joes (page 44)

TUESDAY

BREAKFAST: Tofu Salsa Scramble Breakfast Burrito (page 11)

LUNCH: Kale Quinoa Salad with Sriracha Dressing (page 95)

SNACK: Mango-Blackberry Smoothie (page 168)

DINNER: Fresh Tomato Pasta (page 52)

WEDNESDAY

BREAKFAST: Pressure Cooker Porridge with Toasted Almonds and Jam (page 15)

LUNCH: Club Sandwich (page 158)

SNACK: Everything Chickpeas (page 171)

DINNER: Taco Salad (page 43)

THURSDAY

BREAKFAST: Cherry and Coffee Smoothie Bowl (page 26)

LUNCH: Tomato Soup with Sourdough Croutons (page 48)

SNACK: Rice Crackers with Cream Cheese, Cucumber, and Salsa (page 157)

DINNER: Smoky Bean Chili (page 149)

FRIDAY

BREAKFAST: Yogurt with Warm Blueberry Compote (page 5)

LUNCH: Cold Peanut Noodles (page 116)

SNACK: Green Hummus (page 154)

DINNER: Tomato, Mushroom, and Pepperoncini Pizza (page 119)
and
Old-School Salad (page 64)

SATURDAY

BREAKFAST: French Toast (page 33)

Chia Pudding with Caramelized Bananas (page 20)

LUNCH: Quinoa Patties (page 55)

SNACK: Triscuits with Date Butter and Apples (page 167)

DINNER: Crunchy Vegetable and Peanut Pot Stickers (page 125)
and
Glazed Ginger-Barbecue Tofu (page 126)

DESSERT: Blueberry V'Ice Cream (page 189)

SUNDAY

BRUNCH: Fluffy Pancakes (page 6)

Peanut Butter Granola (page 16)

SNACK: Pita with Za'atar and Cucumber Olive Salad (page 163)

DINNER: Spaghetti and Meatless Balls (page 36)
or
Mushroom Bolognese (page 122)

DESSERT: Chocolate Sheet Cake (page 186)

PREP: Overnight Oats for Monday (page 30)

Acknowledgments

MARK WEINBERG: Photography

MARK SELIGER: Cover photography

MEGAN HEDGPETH: Prop styling

SARA QUESSENBERRY: Food styling and much, much more

LAURA PALESE: Book design

AIMÉE BELL: The dream editor

JENNIFER BERGSTROM: Cheerleader/publisher extraordinaire

RICARDO SOUZA: Everything

Index

Note: Page references in *italics* indicate photographs.

C